GREAT STORIES OF CANADA

SHIPS OF THE GREAT DAYS

GREAT STORIES OF CANADA

Many other titles in preparation

GREAT STORIES OF CANADA

Ships of the Great Days

CANADA'S NAVY IN WORLD WAR II

By JOSEPH SCHULL

ILLUSTRATED BY ED. McNALLY

TORONTO : 1966 : MACMILLAN

Reprinted 1966

Library of Congress Catalog Card No. 62-17716

PRINTED IN CANADA

FOR

JOSEPH CHARLES TRAVERS

Who will be reading it, I hope,
as tales of war recede to join the
mastodon and dinosaur among
the picturesque absurdities of
the past.

Author's Note

This book is an abridgement for younger readers made by the kind permission of the Queen's Printer. The larger work, an official account of Canadian naval operations in the Second World War, was published under the title *The Far Distant Ships* by the Queen's Printer.

Contents

1. Eve of Battle

AUGUST 31, 1939, was a holiday in the port of Vancouver. Two ships of the Canadian navy, the destroyers *Fraser* and *Saint Laurent*, lay in the harbour playing their part in the celebrations. They were, like all destroyers, swift and beautiful greyhounds of the sea. They were nearly two hundred feet long, with dazzling white-painted sides curving gracefully above the water. The slender barrels of two guns pointed forward and two more pointed aft from each deck. Today, on this peaceful holiday, the muzzles were covered with gleaming metal caps. Polished brasswork sparkled in the sunlight, rows of bright-coloured pennants whipped in a light breeze high above the scrubbed decks, and at the gangways officers and seamen in immaculate white greeted the visitors from shore.

Early in the afternoon, however, came a sudden change. Quiet orders passed along the ships' decks. Guests on board were ushered to the gangways; newly-arriving visitors were turned away. The gangways themselves were hauled inboard as the last civilians went ashore. The bright pennants came down, there was an orderly bustle of preparations for sea, and then a churning of water beneath the ships' sterns. They swung for the harbour mouth and within two hours were steaming at full speed for the Panama Canal. A signal from naval headquarters in Ottawa, not unexpected, had turned them from holiday showpieces into ships of war. Beneath their gleaming decks fuel tanks, ammunition magazines, and store-rooms had been well supplied. Their orders were now to "ship warheads and be in all respects ready for action". On September 10 they passed through the Panama Canal, leaving the Pacific Ocean behind them, and turned northward through the Atlantic for Halifax. On the same day Canada went to war with Adolf Hitler's Germany.

The Canadian navy consisted of six destroyers like *Fraser* and *Saint Laurent* and five smaller vessels which were described as "Bangor-class minesweepers". The German navy, with which we were now at war, was twenty times as powerful on the surface and even more dangerous in its undersea forces. Fifty-seven submarines, the dreaded German U-boats, were known to be in operation and two more were being built each month.

The rate of U-boat building would be greatly speeded up with the outbreak of war. Some of the submarines in commission might already have moved to their war stations in the Atlantic. They might be cruising along the ship lanes, low in the water, almost impossible to sight. They might be lying submerged with the eyes of their periscopes poking above the surface, searching for unwary ships, while torpedo men waited below, ready at their tubes. The great German battleships and cruisers might be at sea, ready for a swoop on our harbours and cities along the coast. Any one of the battleships and any two of the cruisers could have blown the entire Canadian navy out of the water.

Between our coasts and the force of this overpowering enemy stood the great shield of England, the Royal Navy. It had always been there. We had grown to nationhood under its protection and had come to accept it and forget it, almost as a fact of geography. There was, however, one disquieting thing to be remembered.

The Royal Navy meant more than ships. It meant bases, without which the ships could not be supplied. It meant shipyards, repair shops, ammunition and weapon factories. The dry-docks and laboratories and testing grounds, the schools in which seamen were trained, the whole vast, centuries-old organization which enabled the ships to move and fight, lay on British soil. Let Britain go down and all this would be lost; not merely lost but much of it in German hands. The ships, such of them as remained, would be hungry and helpless orphans to whom Canada could offer little. Beside us on our own continent was the mighty United States, but it was still neutral, a sleeping giant. It might wake too late, and without it we should face, empty-handed, an Atlantic highway by which our enemy might come when he would.

Britain had to stand. Britain had to be kept alive and powerful. Her life and strength were as vital to us as to her own people. And that island in the north sea, divided from the shores of Europe by the English Channel, lived as she had always lived by sea-borne trade. Without the uninterrupted flow of merchant shipping moving to her ports from all the oceans of the world, Britain would starve.

She had been almost starved by the German U-boats in the First World War. Lying across the ship lanes, sending their torpedoes into hundreds of merchant ships, the submarines of the Kaiser had almost cut off the flow of supplies to England. They had been beaten only when the merchant ships were assembled in great groups and sailed "in convoy" under the protection of warships. Now once again, from the far more deadly undersea navy of Adolf Hitler, the same danger threatened and the same plan must be used to overcome it.

The part which Canada would play in the coming struggle had been settled more than a year before. Halifax, her great Atlantic port, would become the assembly point for convoys moving from North America to the United Kingdom. On the outbreak of war all friendly merchant ships in North American waters would be ordered to break off their voyages and stand in for Halifax. There they would come under the control of the navy. Their captains would receive instructions which were to be obeyed and naval codes which they were expected to learn. They would be ordered to sail in a fixed position in a column of ships, often separated from the ship ahead and the ship astern by not more than a hundred yards, with another column of ships not more than a mile to their left or right. They would have to hold this station in good weather and bad, in daylight and dark, burning no lights at night for fear of attracting U-boats. They would be forbidden to smoke on deck at night. They would be forbidden to throw garbage over the side, since garbage or the gulls which it attracted might give away the convoy's position. They would be able to sail no longer on a direct course chosen by themselves. They would have to move among a huddle of other ships travelling in great roundabout zig-zags planned to throw off a pursuer. Their freedom as independent seamen would pass away from them, for their own safety. And all the responsibility for their men, their vessels, and the thousands of tons of cargo which they carried would descend on the escorting warships.

Most of the warships would be English, but the eleven ships of Canada would play their part too. Many more ships would have to be found, no man knew where as yet. All that was known was that the safety of England and the safety of Canada depended upon the steady coming and going of thousands of merchant vessels. The rhythm of the convoys moving back and forth across the Atlantic would be the heartbeat of the war.

Fraser and *Saint Laurent* arrived in Halifax on September 15, grey ships now and streaked with camouflage. Their gunmuzzles gaped and their men were in the blue of the Atlantic service. *Saguenay*, another of the Canadian destroyers, was waiting for them in the harbour. They found the port crowded with merchant ships summoned in by wireless. They heard masters and owners bewailing the cost of voyages broken off, schedules interrupted, cargoes delayed. Ships' painting parties were busy defiling clean white sides with dingy grey and daubs of camouflage. Merchant officers scowled over pamphlets of convoy instructions and code and signal books more terrible to them than U-boats. Guns were being mounted on the afterdecks of freighters, machine-guns and sub-machine-guns were being issued to the crews. Merchant captains, accustomed to the wide freedom of the seas, were complaining about the impossibility and the absurdity of sailing their cranky vessels nose-to-tail like helpless cows.

And beneath all the grumbling was a surly acceptance of everything that had to be done. The lights had gone out across the world, the seas were no longer open. Men could no longer buy and sell, ship and deliver as they liked. Food and lumber and oil, pig-iron and steel, medicine, machinery, and ammunition – everything by which men lived or fought – must be sent where it was needed without thought of the cost or risk. Sea-borne trade had become a matter of survival, a mighty weapon of war.

The first group of ships had been assembled with rough efficiency and in a surprisingly short time. Others would gather in greater numbers; they were moving toward Halifax now from ports down the American seaboard and around the world. The convoy system was in operation, the plans were being carried out. The remaining question, the question that would hover over all our destinies for the next six years, was starkly simple. Could the ships be got across the Atlantic?

On September 16, one day after *Saint Laurent* arrived, she moved out through the Halifax approaches in company with her sister *Saguenay*. Between the destroyers, waddling eastward with a certain untidy gallantry, were the eighteen merchant ships of Convoy HX-1, Halifax to the United Kingdom.

Awaiting them in the open sea were the British cruisers

Berwick and *York,* and beyond lay the sleety gloom of the Atlantic. A signal-lamp winked out its curt orders from *Berwick*'s bridge. The warships moved to their stations about the two columns of the merchantmen, one ahead, one astern, one on each flank, and the convoy ploughed on. The business of war had begun and it was perhaps as well that the work of watch- and station-keeping left little time to think about the days ahead.

2. The Ships and Men

THE battle upon which the ships of Canada were now embarked was to continue for sixty-eight months, on, above, and beneath the surface of ten million square miles of sea. Before it was ended nearly four hundred vessels wearing the maple leaf would be afloat on the world's oceans and nearly a hundred thousand Canadians would be in service. Their efforts would be combined with the far greater efforts of Britain and the United States, and all together would be barely enough to defeat the forces which a mighty enemy threw against them.

German U-boats, the great threat to the convoys in the Atlantic, had a cruising range of nearly fifteen thousand miles and could remain at sea for as long as three months. They could travel on the surface or they could travel submerged, putting up the long tubes of their periscopes whenever they wanted a view of the surrounding sea. They carried twenty-one torpedoes which could be fired from ranges as

great as seven miles and which would drive through the water at a speed of forty knots, or nearly fifty miles an hour. A U-boat could fire her torpedoes from the surface or from a depth as great as two hundred feet. On the surface she could reach a speed of sixteen knots, and while her speed under water was reduced by about half she would still be travelling faster than the average convoy.

When threatened with attack a U-boat could go into a crash dive which would take her to periscope depth, about twenty feet below the surface, in a little over thirty seconds. Within another minute, still diving downward and twisting away, she would be about 120 feet below and some 700 feet

distant from the swirl where she had gone under.

Even when located, U-boats were very difficult to destroy. They had been specially built to withstand depth-charges, the steel canisters of high explosive which allied ships used against them in the First World War. Within the light outer hull which gave the boat its rakish, graceful lines there was a second "pressure hull" of very tough steel. All the vital parts were enclosed by the pressure hull and were protected by its toughness against tremendous blows. A 300-pound depth-charge, to sink the boat, must be exploded within twenty-one feet. More distant explosions might bring a great gush of oil to the surface, to the delight of an attacking ship, but this was often merely a ruse of U-boat captains who deliberately released the oil. In other cases it might indicate that reserve fuel tanks built into the space between the two hulls had been broken, and such damage meant little. There were U-boats which had been blown to the surface and lifted clear out of the water by depth-charges and yet made their escape and returned to base. These were the powerful and durable weapons of an undersea navy which was already ranging the sea, and which would fight to the bitter end with fanatical determination.

No one realized in September of 1939 how great the struggle would be, nor did anyone dream of the part which Canada would be called on to play. Our five little mine-sweepers were suitable only to patrol our coasts. Our six destroyers, though they could reach speeds of nearly thirty knots, were "short-legged" vessels which carried just enough fuel to cross the Atlantic by the shortest route. It was impossible for them to sail with convoys all the way from Canada to England by the long, zig-zag courses taken to evade the U-boats. It was expected, therefore, that their work would be confined to "local" escort. They would shepherd convoys out from our coast to the high seas where they would be taken over by more powerful ships of the Royal Navy.

So the work began, and so it continued for nearly nine months. On September 17 in mid-afternoon, 353 sea miles to the eastward of Halifax, *Saint Laurent* and *Saguenay* parted company with *Berwick* and *York* and turned back to base. At dusk they passed *Fraser*, outward bound with another convoy. *Skeena*, *Ottawa*, and *Restigouche*, the three other Canadian destroyers, took their turns with succeeding convoys, and by November a seventh destroyer acquired from the Royal Navy and renamed *Assiniboine* was in service.

This first new ship was soon followed by others, for the demands of the war were constantly growing. A few private yachts were purchased to assist the Bangors in patrolling the coasts. Three large luxury liners, *Prince Robert*, *Prince Henry*, and *Prince David*, were taken over from Canadian National Steamships and sent to the dockyards to be stripped down and armed as merchant cruisers. Most important of all, the decision was taken to build a new type of vessel in Canada, specially designed for escort work with the convoys.

The idea for the vessel had come from the whaling ship. Whales, it had been observed, had characteristics in common with the submarine. They could surface suddenly and make off at high speed. When they dived they turned very quickly under water, and the ships which pursued them had to be able to turn as quickly. They frequented stormy and inhospitable waters and the ships of the hunters had to be seaworthy. Moreover, whaling ships were comparatively cheap and simple to build.

As the plans for its building took shape this new type of vessel was given the class-name of "corvette". It was decided that each individual corvette should be named for a Canadian city, as each destroyer was named for a Canadian river, and it was a happy decision. Canada was to build other and better ships before the war ended. Frigates would come from her shipyards, almost as large as her present destroyers. She would build new destroyers more powerful than any she now possessed, and send them to sea wearing the names of her Indian tribes. But no ships would leave a prouder memory than her hundred and twenty corvettes, those small, squat, ugly children of the whaling ship, which were to jog on, year in, year out, by the side of the crawling convoys.

The new ships were still plans on paper or keels on a slipway as the war moved into the winter of 1940. It would be almost a year before any of them were ready, yet the need was becoming desperate as the overworked destroyers and patrol craft tried to cope with ever-expanding duties. Ships sailing on local escort spent from two and a half to three days at sea on each voyage. Frequently they were called on to make two voyages a week. Merchant ships in the crowded convoys were often damaged by wild weather or collision and had to be helped to harbour. A constant watch had to be maintained against attacks by U-boats or surface ships which did not come but which were possible at any time. No Canadian warship had crossed the Atlantic as yet and none had seen an enemy, but the sea miles and the hours of sea time left their mark on the faces of the ships' companies. They were tired men, these hard-bitten sailors of the permanent force and the reserve, and there were never enough of them even for the few ships we had. But a first trickle of new-comers, fresh-faced and self-conscious in their round caps and bell-bottomed trousers, was now beginning to find its way to the ports.

They were the vanguard of thousands more, and they came from the training depots which the Royal Canadian Naval Volunteer Reserve had set up in all the principal Canadian cities. They were lads from school, lads from the towns and cities and farms across the country. Many of them had never smelt the sea before. They had been given a hasty three months' training in seamanship, rifle drill and general naval discipline. They had been taught a little about handling boats and tying knots. They had practised signalling with lights and flags in the Morse code. They had learned that the fo'c'sle was the forward end of a ship, that the quarter-deck was aft, and that the port side was on the left hand and the starboard on the right. They had learned to wear the round cap square on their heads and to fold their bell-bottomed trousers neatly into the seven pleats that stood for the seven seas. Now, with their hammocks and duffle bags, in little groups of ten or a dozen, they trooped up the gangways of the destroyers, saluted, and entered on the life of the sea.

It was a hard and confusing life at first, with a burly coxswain barking at your heels and a divisional officer looking you over, remote and stern. A man stumbled down the companion-way into the seamen's mess and found himself with six square feet of space in which to swing the hammock which no sailor ever called anything but a "mick". He found himself with a locker for all his possessions and a rack in which to stow his mick, neatly lashed into a hard roll with mattress and blankets inside when it was not in use. He was issued with his sea boots and his duffle coat. He got his plate and cup and knife and fork and spoon for the meals he would draw from the cook and eat at the long table in the mess. Then he was assigned to his watch, and work began.

The watches divided the day into five periods of four hours each and two periods of two hours each, which were called "dog-watches". Twice each day a man stood his trick with the rest of the men assigned to his watch, acting as the eyes and brains and hands of the ship. Then he was off duty, but he was never idle. The shrill "Wakey-Wakey" piped through the mess each morning at 7.15, followed by the "Rise and Shine", and the off-duty men piled out of their hammocks. Then came the "Lash and Stow" and the rolled-up hammocks went to the racks as the men of the morning watch, who had been on duty since four o'clock, came trooping down for their breakfast and their sleep. The men of the forenoon watch were already off to relieve them, and for the rest of the ship's company the endless routine of training and housekeeping began.

There was always cleaning, painting, scrubbing, and repair work to be done. The smart, shore-going uniforms were folded away in the locker. You spent your time in a turtle-neck sweater and rough blue work-pants – "dungarees" – all too often with the pants rolled up to the knees and a mop and scrub-bucket in your hands. No part of the ship, you soon discovered, was ever clean enough to suit the Captain or the First Lieutenant, and the work-parties went everywhere. You soon became familiar with the clanging steel corridors and the watertight doors which could be shut in an emergency to close off damaged parts of the ship. The steep companion-ways leading from deck to deck took you at a clattering run from the freshness of the harbour air into the steamy heat of the engine-room and the boiler-room deep beneath the water. There you looked round at the maze of generators and turbines and pipes and dials and drive-shafts and wondered if you would ever know what any of them were for.

If you were to be a stoker you would soon have to learn.

Whatever your "rating" was to be – and it might be stoker, gunner, signalman, seaman or any of half a dozen other branches – you would soon know your way about. You would have inspected the lifeboats on their davits and the "carley floats", or life-rafts, lashed on the after deck. You would have looked at the cranes and windlasses for raising heavy gear, at the capstan for bringing up the anchor, and the housing where the anchor was secured. You would know that the officers' cabins were aft, with the ward room where they took their meals. You would have been up to the bridge, looking forward over the fo'c'sle, from which the captain or the officer of the watch directed the ship when it was at sea. You would know the wheel-house below the bridge, where the helmsman steered. You would have seen, and probably you would have polished, the brass mouths of the speaking-tubes which led down from the bridge to the wheel-house and the engine-room to carry the captain's orders. You would have watched the yeoman of signals, always on duty on the bridge, "talking" to other ships in the harbour with his big signalling lamp or his flags or running up some of the pennants which were stored in their neat rack beside him. You would have seen the ammunition magazines and the hoists which sent up the shells. You would have seen the cable lockers and the machine shops and the carpenter's shop and the sick bay and the store-rooms. You would have begun to realize that these graceful steel sides which you had admired from shore housed an immensely complicated, eternally watchful beehive of the sea.

But there would be much more than that, for the aim of everything that was done was to weld ship and men into a weapon of war. There was constant drill in seamanship, in signalling, in fire-fighting and damage control. For hours each day the long barrels of the guns in their two turrets fore and aft were raised and lowered, swung right, swung left, as the gun-crews snapped through their drill. The dummy shells came up with the hoist, the breeches of the guns swung open, the shells were rammed home. The aiming-wheels spun and stopped, the breeches opened again, the shells came out and the whole process was repeated, always with

more speed, always with more precision. This was a business where, when the shells were live and the target an enemy, every second would count.

It was the same with the smaller guns mounted about the ship, and it was the same with the depth-charges. You saw real depth-charges for the first time now, those round canisters in rails along the quarter-deck, filled with their hundreds of pounds of high explosive. You raced round under the eyes of barking officers, learning to operate the throwers

which would send the charges hurtling down through the water after a U-boat. Even in the first days on board, and even while the ship lay in harbour, you began to feel a little of the iron discipline and fierce urgency of the war.

Finally, if you were a rating chosen for the work, you would be taken to the little cabin opening off the bridge and introduced to "asdic". Asdic was the great secret weapon with which the Royal Navy had entered the war, and it had proved to be a shattering surprise for the U-boats. It was a listening and finding device, as simple in its principle as a shout and an echo. The idea was to send a beam of sound through the water, which would send back an echo when it made contact with a U-boat's hull, in the same way that a shout comes back when it bounces off the steep wall of a cliff. Officers of the Royal Navy, working secretly for many years, had found a way not only to send out a beam and recover an echo, but also to locate and follow the object which produced the echo.

When the asdic operator sat down in the cabin off the bridge he had before him a set of knobs and dials. He had also a frame holding paper ruled into small squares over which an electric needle would travel when he pressed a button. He put on the head-phones and pressed the button. From a small, egg-shaped dome under the ship's hull an electronic beam travelled out through the water for a mile or more, swinging back and forth in an arc which the operator could control. When it struck an object under water the steady "buzz-buzz-buzz" of the outgoing beam was interrupted. The echo came back, a curious, high-keyed "ping" which kept sounding as long as the operator held contact with the object. If the object moved, the needle moved across the face of the squared paper, making the "asdic plot" which showed the object's position. It was not always a U-boat – it might be an old wreck lying on the bottom, or a floating timber with metal trailing from it. Sometimes even a school of fish might send back an echo. But a trained man could usually distinguish the "ping" of the beam against the hull of a U-boat, and could follow it as it tried to escape, reporting its position, its depth in the water, and the direction in which it was moving.

As you looked for the first time at the lighted face of the asdic plot, and listened to the beam and heard the officer explaining how it worked, the thought of the U-boats began to seem a little less terrible. Deadly as they were, you would not be fighting them entirely blind. You were warned that asdic was not a perfect defence. It could seldom find an enemy on the surface. Even beneath the surface the U-boats were already trying methods to counteract it. They would often succeed, but quite as often they would fail. The perils of the weird battle were more nearly equal now. Your ship would sail with guns and throwers ready and the asdic searching about it, never quite secure. The men of the under-sea navy would move beneath you, always with the thought of those fingers of sound reaching out to grasp them, never knowing when the spaced, uncanny, high-pitched tapping of the beam against their hulls would bring the plunging thud of depth-charges.

There was never time enough in harbour to learn much about asdic or anything else. Training and fighting must go hand in hand. Before a new man had been many days on board the pipes whistled through the ship with the call for the cable-party to fall in and the sea dutymen to muster. The anchor came up and was secured, or the lines tying the ship to a jetty were cast off. The jack-staff which had carried the flag at the forepeak came down to clear the field for the guns. The men of the duty watch lined up on the fo'c'sle-head as the ship steered out of the harbour. You felt the first sway of motion, and the breeze from the harbour mouth began to grow salty and wet. Then came the swell of the Atlantic itself. If you were sailing with a convoy there would be a jumble of ships somewhere off in the distance and a winking of signals from many lamps. If you were alone there would be only the curt flash from the port war-signal station giving the captain his last orders. And then, unbelievably, you were at sea in war.

The strangeness of it all would wear off after a few voyages. If you were a look-out on the bridge the captain and the officers of the watch would become familiar figures. You would hear their quiet orders passed down through the speaking-tubes. You would begin to make some sense of their work. You would become used to sailing beside the ragged lines of slow merchantmen, keeping them in station, urging on the stragglers, and sometimes turning off in darkness and wild weather to hunt for a ship which had broken down or strayed. You would grow hardened to the nights of snow and sleet and fog, to the tossing of the ship, to the headaches and retchings of sea-sickness. You would become accustomed to the harsh buzz of the "action-stations" signal, sending each man racing to his post at dawn and dusk. You would even become a little bored with it all. But you would never be allowed to forget that a time might come when "action stations" would be more than a routine precaution. You would never grow too hardened to remember, as you stood on look-out sweeping the sea with your binoculars, that each low ripple on the water might be the hump of the conning tower above the hull of a surfaced U-boat, that each twist of foam might be the feather of a periscope wake, and that any moment might bring the roar and flash of an exploding torpedo.

The hours of the middle watch, from midnight to four in the morning, would be the hardest at first. In that cold darkness with not a light to be seen and only the vague blots of the merchantmen in the distance a man's blood ran slower and his courage sank. The flimsy life-jacket round your shoulders gave little comfort when you remembered the tales you heard of men gone down in the sunken ships, or even of the men rescued. Some of them had come back to Halifax from torpedoings far out in the Atlantic, maimed by explosions, choked with oil spreading out over the sea from shattered tanks, with feet and hands frozen from hours in the icy water. And these were the lucky ones who had found rafts or lifeboats or bits of wreckage to cling to, or who had climbed up along a ship's side by "scramble-nets" dropped from the deck. You thought of the few boats and rafts and nets which your own ship carried, thought of that water speckled with white faces and bobbing heads, and wondered what your own chances would be.

And yet sometimes after a few voyages the middle watch had its good hours too. The throbbing of the engines and the swish of the backwash along the ship's sides were familiar sounds now; you were at home with them. You were at home with your mates, the other look-outs on the bridge, the look-outs on the quarter-deck, the men shivering in their duffle coats by the guns, the off-watch men asleep in the mess, and the stokers deep below you in the shining jungles of the engine-room and the boiler-room. In the wireless-room the communications men listened to a clatter of signals from around the world, waiting for a message to the ship. The helmsman swung his wheel to the orders from the bridge, the asdic men in their head-phones sat alert. You knew them all and you knew your job now, as they knew theirs. You could depend on them and you were a part of them, a part of your country at war. You were a part of this ship and you were finding, little by little, that the ship had grown to be a part of you.

3. British Waters

IN Halifax harbour, on the afternoon of May 24, 1940, *Restigouche, Skeena,* and *Saint Laurent* were preparing to go to sea. They were salt-stained and battered from a hard winter of local escort work. The mess-deck "buzz" – the daily crop of rumours and gossip – promised nothing more than a few days' sailing with another convoy. Each day the radio and the newspapers brought more depressing news of the fighting on land. Hitler had invaded Norway, Holland, Belgium, and France. It seemed certain that in a few weeks all Europe would be at his feet. Hundreds of merchantmen and hundreds of thousands of tons of cargo had been sent to the bottom in the waters around the British Isles, but no U-boat had yet appeared within range of a Canadian ship. The war had begun to seem a thing of drab, relentless monotony which was being fought and lost on the other side of the world. The men in the destroyers felt gloomy, helpless, and far away from the battle as their ships nosed out of harbour and they looked about for their convoy.

There was no convoy to be seen, and this time there would be no turning back to Halifax after a day or two at sea. The course of the ships was set direct for England. An urgent signal had arrived in Ottawa the day before, requesting every destroyer which Canada could spare. Hitler's armies were sweeping along the western coast of France. They faced Britain now across the narrow ribbon of the English Channel and invasion was possible at any time.

Restigouche, Skeena, and *Saint Laurent* arrived in Plymouth on June 1. *Fraser* followed them on June 3. Canadian sailors were now in the heart of the war zone. The boredom of Halifax had been suddenly exchanged for a turmoil of disaster and defeat. The ships had barely time to mount the high-angle guns they would need against the patrol planes and dive-bombers of the German *Luftwaffe* before they were steaming south for the Bay of Biscay. Here, along the Biscay coast of France, towers of flame and smoke climbed above the advancing German armies. Thousands of allied soldiers and more thousands of refugees were streaming down the coast ahead of them, hoping for escape from the few remaining seaports. Our destroyers became part of a great rescue force of allied ships, and it was in this work, on the night of June 25, that the first blow fell.

Restigouche, Fraser, and British ships had been helping a fleet of merchantmen to evacuate the little port of Saint-Jean de Luz, far down the French coast toward the Spanish border. They had almost finished at dusk when field-guns, appearing on the high hills above the town, put an end to the work. The harbour was quickly cleared of the merchant ships, and as the last of them steamed out *Fraser* and *Resti-gouche* put to sea under the orders of the British cruiser *Calcutta*.

It was now about ten o'clock in the evening, with a fresh breeze lifting the sea into a moderate swell and light clouds drifting across the moon. *Fraser* was a mile and a half from *Calcutta*, in position on her starboard bow, that is, to the right of her and a little ahead. The station of *Restigouche* was on the cruiser's port quarter, which meant that she was a mile and a half to the left of her and a little astern. All three ships were travelling at high speed with the possibility of attack by submarine or from the air at any time. They had been in continuous action for nearly a week and few of their men, least of all their commanding officers, had had more than one full night's sleep in the past ten.

As the ships steamed on, just visible to each other in the darkness, the signal for "line ahead" winked from *Calcutta's* bridge. The destroyers were to form in a single line behind the cruiser, and *Fraser* altered course to obey. Her command-ing officer's intention was to turn inward toward *Calcutta*, run back down to starboard of her, and come into station astern. *Calcutta*, however, as she saw *Fraser* begin the turn, thought that the ship was crossing ahead of her to run down the other side. She was travelling so fast that this would have been risky and she therefore swung sharply away to star-board, sounding a blast on her siren.

The misunderstanding left both ships steering straight for each other, with their combined speeds closing the gap at something like fifty miles an hour. *Calcutta's* signal-blast was *Fraser's* first warning, and it was already too late. The ships covered the last two hundred yards separating them in less than eleven seconds and *Calcutta*, still swinging to starboard, sheared her way through the forward part of *Fraser*. The destroyer's fo'c'sle broke clean off, turned over, and floated away bottom up. Her bridge, with the captain and men about him, was lifted onto *Calcutta*'s bow and remained there, heaving and groaning with the shock.

Restigouche had moved into station about a mile astern of *Calcutta*. With the crash of the collision she raced up alongside *Fraser* and worked herself in toward the after part of the broken ship. Rocking in the swell which threatened to dash her against the jagged mass of steel, *Restigouche* brought her stern round to touch the stern of *Fraser*. While the two hulls ground together, sixty of *Fraser*'s crew, most of them bruised and shocked, climbed over the tossing stern rails to the deck of the sister ship. Many other men had been thrown into the water, and for these both *Restigouche* and the damaged *Calcutta* lowered their boats, dropped their carley floats, and let down the scramble-nets along their sides.

Fraser's overturned fore part had floated away with men still clinging to its jagged sides. *Restigouche*, coming up from astern in the darkness, had at first mistaken it for a half-submerged wreck. When she realized what it was she tried to work up alongside, but just as she drew near the whole mass of twisted steel leaned over and sank. More men went tumbling down its sides into the water. Oil began to spread out over the surface, choking off their cries, and there was an hour of desperate turmoil and confusion. The boat-crews of the ships managed to rescue sixteen officers and 134 men.

Forty-seven Canadian and nineteen British sailors were lost.

Fraser was our first casualty and it was a heavy blow, but it was only an incident of those disastrous days. The United Kingdom was surrounded by an overpowering enemy and was undergoing such an assault from the air as men had never known before. Sixteen thousand of her people were dead and twenty thousand wounded from mass raids which seemed to be battering her cities and seaports into powder. Her beaten armies had come home from Dunkirk with all their weapons lost. Worse still, the slender channels of reinforcement by sea, which were her only hope, seemed likely to be cut at any moment.

The "Western Approaches" were a few close-grouped sea-lanes leading to British ports. Every day ships came and went through them in hundreds and it was here, in these narrow and congested areas, that the German U-boats and the German planes concentrated their attacks. By the end of June they had made it impossible for ships to enter the ports of southern England. Only the northern harbours remained, and even the convoys steering for them through misty seas round the north of Ireland were savagely attacked.

Skeena and *Restigouche* were the first Canadians to join with British ships in the battle for the island sea-lanes. Later came *Saint Laurent, Ottawa,* and *Saguenay.* It was a battle with few victories. The ships were always at sea, summoned from convoy to convoy and from new disaster to new attack. They saw the work of the U-boats but seldom a U-boat itself. German planes swooped down on them from lowering skies, day after day they came on sinking ships and drowning men. They brought damaged vessels to port and rescued hundreds

of survivors, but for months the chance to strike a blow in return eluded them.

For *Saint Laurent* the first and largest rescue of the summer had its grimly ironic side. On the morning of July 2 she was ordered to a position where the liner *Arandora Star* had been torpedoed. She arrived to find more than eight hundred men floundering in the water, clinging to pieces of wreckage or cramming a half-dozen lifeboats which were scattered miles apart on the horizon. Almost every man of them was a German or an Italian, for *Arandora Star* had been carrying enemy civilians arrested in England and bound to Canada for internment.

Saint Laurent steamed slowly into the oily wilderness of sea and lowered her boats. As the boats pulled away and began to move among the hundreds of bobbing heads, the destroyer worked herself alongside the groups of men clinging to rafts and the larger pieces of wreckage. Most of the survivors were exhausted and could do little to help themselves. *Saint Laurent's* men had to go over the side after them. For hour after hour Canadian sailors, hip-deep in water, balanced on rafts or crates or pieces of timber as they passed lines round limp bodies whose weight was nearly doubled by their wet and oil-soaked clothing. Lying often with engines stopped and with no protection from U-boat or air attacks, the destroyer gathered in the men from the water and waited for the return of her own boats and the boats of *Arandora Star*. She turned for port at last with every bunk and hammock and every inch of space above or below decks crammed with citizens of the countries with which she was at war.

A lone British patrol plane had passed over the scene while rescue work was going on. "Most of these people are Germans or Italians," *Saint Laurent* had signalled him. "How bloody funny," came the comment from his lamp as he wheeled away.

It was five months later, on December 1, that *Saint Laurent* sighted her first U-boat. It appeared a mile away on her starboard bow, surfaced but already diving. *Saint Laurent* bore down on the widening swirl where the German had disappeared, passed over the position, and began her asdic search. The "ping" came, and the pencil wavered across the face of her asdic plot, showing the movements of the enemy as he made off beneath the surface. *Saint Laurent* followed deliberately, careful not to drop her depth-charges too soon for fear the explosions would disturb the echo. The British destroyer *Viscount* appeared on the horizon. *Saint Laurent* hoisted the black pennant which signalled that she was hunting a U-boat and waited till *Viscount* came up. The British ship reported a confirming echo. Then, with the unseen target firmly held by the asdic beams, the two ships began the slow dance of death which is a deliberate depth-charge attack.

Viscount steamed along the wavering course of the submarine beneath, stalking it at a distance of some 1,200 yards. *Saint Laurent*, running in approximately at right-angles to *Viscount*'s course, came directly over the U-boat's position. A word of command from her bridge was echoed by a series of orders rapped out on her quarter-deck, and for the men of her depth-charge party the weary months of training and waiting became suddenly worth while. Two steel canisters rolled along the rails and dropped in the water astern. The light bark of the port and starboard throwers followed, and four more canisters hurtled into the air and plunged to the sea, two on each side and about sixty-five yards out from the ship. Two more charges rolled from the stern rails as the destroyer passed on, then two more. A few seconds later there came a series of muffled explosions from the depths. Fountains of water mushroomed in the sea and the ship's whole frame shuddered to the impact. *Saint Laurent* had "laid her eggs", a diamond-shaped pattern of ten depth-charges falling in pairs at spaced intervals. One charge of each was "heavy", set to explode beneath the U-boat, the other "light" to explode above.

With her charges away, the Canadian ship came round to take over *Viscount's* position as stalker astern of the submarine. *Viscount* moved in from the side as *Saint Laurent* had done, and fired her charges. Then *Saint Laurent* took over again, and the relentless hammering continued for three hours, guided back and forth above the squirming enemy by the incessant "ping" of the asdic beam. Eighty charges carrying twelve tons of explosive had gone down when oil began coming to the surface and the contact faded out. It was a "probably sunk", a slightly unsatisfying victory, but the best we had yet had.

One day later *Saint Laurent's* sister, *Saguenay*, was limping for port, a torpedoed cripple. She had been escorting a convoy when, about four o'clock in the morning, a flare shot up from the dark sea astern of her. It had been fired by a U-boat a mile or so off, and as *Saguenay* came round and opened fire a torpedo ripped into her port side.

The seamen's mess was instantly ablaze, and the flames soon rose so fiercely that the entire fore part of the ship had to be cleared. Then smoke and flame forced the captain and the men of the watch to leave the bridge. Paints and oils in the paint shop caught fire next, and salt water, pouring through a jagged gash in the ship's side, set off calcium flares which fed their choking fumes into the general inferno.

Fire-parties attempting to make headway against the blaze were beaten back. There was nothing for it but to flood the forward ammunition magazine, where shells might soon be exploded by the heat. As tons of water poured down into the magazine the entire fore part of the ship, for some sixty feet back from the bow, began to bend toward the water. Cables and heavy gear rattled overside and then, as a great section of the smashed hull broke off and sank, the blazing fo'c'sle tilted upward again.

The wrecked ship was lighting the sea for miles around her and any moment might bring another torpedo, but the engineers and stokers remained at their posts through it all. When the British destroyer *Highlander* arrived about an hour later *Saguenay* was moving at a speed of two knots, steered from the emergency position at the after end. For the rest of the night and most of the next day her crew continued to fight the fires. By early evening, after fifteen desperate hours, the fires were smouldering down and the ship had worked up her speed to six knots. At noon the next day she rounded the north of Ireland and three days later she reached a British port. Twenty-one of her men had been killed and eighteen wounded.

4. Widening War

Saguenay was now out of action and *Fraser* had been lost. The battle in British waters had cost our navy twenty-five per cent of its strength. In warmer waters far to the south, however, two other Canadian ships were coming into service and one had already given a good account of herself.

Prince Robert came out of Esquimalt dockyards in September of 1940 with all the trimmings of a luxury liner cut away and with heavy guns mounted on her forward and after decks. She was now an armed merchant cruiser, and her first orders were to sail for the port of Manzanillo in Mexico. Here *Weser* was lying, a German merchant ship which had taken refuge in the neutral port at the outbreak of war and which was now known to be making preparations for sea. *Prince Robert* was to patrol off the port to intercept her, keeping out of sight during the day and closing in at night.

After dark on September 25 she sighted a freighter nosing out of Manzanillo Bay. It was *Weser* and she had not yet seen *Prince Robert*. She was just clear of the harbour break-water, however, and could still turn back if she were alarmed. To the south of the harbour there was a lighthouse standing on a high hill. *Prince Robert* ran as close inshore as she dared and crawled along by the lighthouse, keeping in the shadow of the hill. The master of the German ship did see a faint blot in the darkness behind him, but did not realize that it was in motion and took it for an island. He continued sea-ward and within a few minutes *Prince Robert* had cut him off from land.

She could not make her capture, however, until the German was outside the three-mile limit of neutral waters. *Weser* moved on with the dark shape of *Prince Robert* crawling in her wake. The ship's company watched silently from action stations. At length, as the three-mile limit was passed, the warship churned up on the German's port quarter. Her searchlight cut a blinding swath through the darkness, startled shouts rose from *Weser's* deck, and the ship came to a stop. A Canadian boarding-party, armed to the teeth, swarmed on board of her, knocked down the few men who attempted to resist, and had the ship securely in their possession within ten minutes. The white ensign rose above the swastika flag, and our first capture of the war had been made.

Prince Henry saw even livelier action than her sister ship, but was not quite so lucky. She came out of the dockyard in February of 1941 and sailed for the South Pacific to take up station off Callao, Peru. Here she was to serve under the orders of the British cruiser *Diomede*. Two other German merchant ships, *Hermonthis* and *Muenchen*, had taken refuge in Callao and were expected to sail shortly. *Prince Henry* and *Diomede* were there to capture them.

Diomede was called away in the middle of March after a watch which had gone on for three weeks. By March 24 the Germans were still in harbour. *Prince Henry* sailed into the port too and took on a supply of provisions which she did not need. Her real intention was to have a look at the German ships, listen to the gossip of the harbour, and try to find out what they were likely to do. They had taken on all the fuel they could carry and seemed to be ready for a long voyage. The dock-side workers said the ships had been wired with explosive charges and were ready to destroy themselves if there was a risk of capture. When they broke out of harbour, it was believed, they would separate and try to run for Japan on different courses.

Prince Henry's captain decided to put to sea and disappear, hoping to tempt the Germans out. He remained well off the port for ten days, cruising in a wide arc, and at last the expected signal reached him. *Hermonthis* and *Muenchen* had sailed.

Prince Henry was then some sixty miles south of Callao. She put back toward the port at full speed and eight hours later she sighted *Muenchen*, fifteen miles away. The German had sighted *Prince Henry* at the same moment and he swung away to the west. He could only make eleven knots, however, and *Prince Henry* was racing after him at twenty. In forty minutes the fifteen-mile gap had narrowed to about eight and *Muenchen* was in range of the Canadian guns. *Prince*

Henry flashed the signal, "Stop instantly or I will open fire."
Muenchen continued on her course and a shell screamed
across her bows and splashed in the water beside her. The
answer was a cloud of smoke from the deck of the merchantman as her demolition charges were set off. Then the crew
climbed into their boats, lowered them to the water and
pulled away for the coast. By the time *Prince Henry* drew
alongside *Muenchen*, the ship was a mass of flame and there
was no possibility of saving her.

Hermonthis however, was still on the run, and *Prince
Henry* swung off to the south in search of her. Four and a half

hours later smoke lifted above the horizon. The enemy ship was already on fire and putting down boats. *Prince Henry* ran for her, and as she drew near lowered her launch with a boarding-party to round up the German crew. After a brief chase through the smoke around the ship one of the boats was captured. Some grim-looking Canadian sailors, with rifles and bayonets and sub-machine-guns, forced a dozen reluctant Nazis to climb back on board *Hermonthis* with them.

The ship was heavily on fire but there seemed to be a chance of saving her. The first thing was to close the sea-cocks, the valves deep down in the engine-room which had been opened to flood the ship. This was done, with Germans moving ahead at the points of Canadian bayonets to show the way. Then *Prince Henry* tied herself to the weather side of *Hermonthis* – the side from which the wind was blowing – and turned all her hoses on the flames. More of her men came swarming over the side to fight the fires in the holds, but the pumps of the German ship had been put out of action and nothing could be done without them in the crowded cargo space. The fight had to be given up after four hours. *Prince Henry*'s singed and smoke-blackened sailors came trooping back to her decks, pushing their prisoners ahead of them. The ship cast off her lines and drew back half a mile to point-blank range. Then her guns opened up and *Hermonthis* went to the bottom.

In the war to the north other ships were now being added to the Canadian navy, and thousands of men were coming to the ports to man them. Six destroyers came to us from the United States in the autumn of 1941, and by the winter they were in British waters. A dozen of our new corvettes had also arrived, and were looked at curiously by men of the larger ships. They were little more than half the size of a destroyer, they were dumpy and squat, and the highest speed they could reach was about seventeen knots. Their mess decks were small and cramped, their men lived a crowded, wet, uncomfortable life, but somehow few men complained. They seemed already to have confidence in their little vessels and almost an affection for them, and the feeling began to be shared by older men as they watched the corvettes with a convoy or two.

The ships were seaworthy and they were right for their job. They did not have to be fast to keep up with the slow merchantmen but they did have to be able to turn quickly and weave in and out among the convoy columns. They did this amazingly well. Their "turning-circle" was very small, they could spin round as fast as a U-boat on the surface, and if they could not quite keep pace with it when it went flat out they could at least drive it away from the merchant ships. They carried a four-inch gun forward and smaller guns aft, they were equipped with asdic and depth-charges, and to a U-boat under water they were as deadly as a destroyer.

They had come from the shipyards none too soon, and they were not to be long in British waters. The battle was growing fiercer and it was spreading outward from the Western Approaches. The undersea navy was increasing all the time and it was attacking by new methods. Few submarines now waited submerged for a convoy to pass near them. They rode surfaced and awash during the day, with their conning towers just above the water, following the convoy's course at a distance of perhaps ten miles. At night they gathered in "wolf-packs" of as many as a dozen boats and came in from the darkest side to launch their torpedoes and make off at high speed. Asdic could seldom detect them on the surface, and even when they were sighted it was usually too late. The torpedoes would have struck home, merchant ships would be ablaze and sinking. The escorting warships had the rest of the convoy to think of and could not leave it to go far in pursuit.

The U-boat which first sighted a convoy might follow it for days, giving no sign of its presence except a curt wireless signal which might be intercepted by an allied operator. This was the sighting report which went to Lorient, the U-boat control centre on the German-held coast of France. Lorient received all sighting reports, Lorient moved all boats to the area where it wished an attack to be made, and only when the pack was fully gathered did the order come to go in.

It was proving to be a terribly effective system, and more and more now the attacks were moving out into the middle and western Atlantic. Here convoys could be intercepted far from the British Isles and beyond the range of most short-legged escort vessels. It began to be clear to allied planners that a new move must be made on the vast checker-board of the ocean.

The first move was to base a force of British escort vessels on the ports of Iceland. Here, along the cold northern routes which the ships had now to take, they were a thousand miles to the west of Britain and could bring convoys home from the middle Atlantic. But Iceland was not enough. Another base and another force was required, far to the west and well out from Halifax. This force could take over the convoys as they came out from Halifax under local escort and bring them to mid-ocean where British ships would meet them. The base chosen was St. John's, Newfoundland, five hundred miles nearer to the United Kingdom than Halifax, and the force chosen was the Canadian navy.

Early in June, therefore, with the battle in British waters still at its height, all the ships of Canada turned westward again. They were to be based once more on their own side of the ocean and were to sail from St. John's as the ships of the Newfoundland Escort Force.

5. The Western Atlantic

SYDNEY, Nova Scotia, had now become a second port of assembly for convoys, and on August 30, 1941, Convoy SC-42 moved out of the harbour bound for England. It consisted of sixty-four slow freighters which would sail at an average speed of about seven knots. It was spread out in nine columns over twenty-five square miles of sea. Cramming the cargoholds and piled high on the decks of its ships were well over half a million tons of war supplies.

The ships of the local escort formed about it and the long grey lines crawled north and eastward to a point about two hundred miles off the coast of Newfoundland. Here, awaiting them low on the horizon, were four other ships. They were the destroyer *Skeena* and the corvettes *Orillia*, *Kenogami*, and *Alberni*. They had sailed from St. John's and were now to take over the mid-ocean voyage as ships of the Newfoundland Escort Force.

Signals flashed from the bridge of *Skeena*, the senior ship.

She moved to the head of the convoy as the local escort turned back for Sydney. *Orillia* took station astern, *Alberni* moved out to starboard, and *Kenogami* began her slow, zig-zagging course along the port side. Each ship moved with its asdic sweeping in a wide arc, and the four of them together were supposed to provide a complete circle of protection about the merchant vessels. Their men knew that they did not. They were far too few to make a complete search of the great area of sea covered by the convoy, but in these days there were never enough ships. Sailors and merchant seamen alike did what they could and hoped for the best. For seven days the convoy ploughed on, still north and east, up into the high latitudes around Cape Farewell and the tip of Greenland.

Wireless operators on watch in the ships had already begun to pick up German U-boat signals. They were in code and could not be read but they were certainly sighting reports going to Lorient, and Lorient was replying with many more signals. By the seventh day the air was filled with them, and it was clear that a wolf-pack was gathering. The convoy swung due north, running in dangerously near to the Greenland coast in an attempt to throw off the shadowers. At dusk, however, the dull roar of an explosion was heard from one of the columns. The merchant ship *Muneric*, her belly blown out by a torpedo, sank like a stone.

Kenogami, on the port side of the convoy, had seen the glistening wake of the torpedo coming from astern of her. She turned back in the gathering darkness and began a zig-zagging "sweep" along its track. Off her starboard bow another torpedo churned by, just missing her. At the same moment she sighted the U-boat on the surface, a thousand yards away, making for the Greenland coast. She opened fire and gave chase, but a flash from *Skeena's* signal-lamp recalled her. Another U-boat had appeared at the head of the convoy. Ten minutes later a third was sighted. Five minutes after that a fourth conning tower cut through the water, inside the convoy, racing down between the columns. Just as it was sighted a torpedo went home in a second merchant ship, and a minute later a volcano of flame and wreckage leaped from an oil-tanker as she blew up.

There were at least eight submarines attacking. *Skeena* and her corvettes were outnumbered two to one. Men from the torpedoed ships were choking in the oily water, but the first duty of the escort was to fight off the enemy. The work of rescue, if it could be done at all, had to be left to the other merchant vessels. Some of the ships did stop, but for the most part the lumbering columns of the convoy swept on. Every ship which stopped or turned out of station risked collision with another ship. The lagging vessel became an almost certain target for a U-boat. Each merchant captain had his own ship to think of and had to weigh the lives of his own men against the chance of saving others. As they swept by blazing wrecks or the dark swirl in the water where a ship had disappeared, the destroyer and the corvettes dropped all their own carley floats. Here and there they stopped for a moment and lowered their scramble-nets among clusters of drowning men. Each stop, however, was instantly broken off as a stream of bright-coloured tracer bullets whipping out from one of the merchant ships warned of another sighting.

Until midnight a high white moon silhouetted the vessels like so many ducks riding the bands of a shooting-gallery. Seven ships, with their thousands of tons of steel and grain and fuel-oil, went hissing through the black fathoms to the bottom. An eighth, the tanker *Tahchee*, had also been torpedoed and had fallen far astern. *Orillia* was trying to save it, so that the escorts about the convoy were now reduced to three.

A little after midnight a cloud-bank moved in from the north-east and covered the moon. The merciful blackness gave the convoy a chance to alter course in the hope of throwing off the U-boats. The warning that a turn was to be made was signalled down the columns of ships. Then, five minutes before the actual order for the turn was given, came another stream of machine-gun tracers from the deck of a merchant ship. They were aimed at a U-boat which was inside the convoy and running up one of the lanes.

Skeena cut into the convoy and raced up the lane after the U-boat. The German, still well ahead, swung at a right-angle, crossed the line of ships, turned sharply again, and ran in the opposite direction down the next lane. *Skeena* and the U-boat passed each other going in opposite directions with a column of merchantmen between them. A minute later the German's conning tower dipped and he slid out of sight in a crash-dive.

Almost at that moment, with the moon hidden and full blackness on the sea, the convoy made its turn. *Skeena*, in the midst of it, was trapped among the huge, swinging shapes of the merchantmen. One of them loomed suddenly on her out of the dark and she put her engines to full astern, avoiding the crash by inches. Sliding and weaving among the other ships, she made her way at last to the outside and took up the battle again. A mile away another merchantman was hit, sending a gush of orange-coloured flame a hundred feet into the sky. It became a cone of fire and smoke, rising to a point and spreading out into a curious downy-looking cushion. One of *Skeena's* men stood watching among the depth-charge party on the quarter-deck, idle for a moment as the ship raced through the water. "I could sit on it!" he heard himself saying to his mate.

Morning came and the U-boats drew off for a time. Just at noon, however, a torpedo struck the merchantman *Thistle-glen*. The vessel shuddered, up-ended slowly and went down, taking a cargo of steel and pig-iron to the bottom. This time *Skeena* had sighted a periscope and was already over the spot where it had disappeared. She dropped a pattern of depth-charges and came in again, listening on her asdic. The contact was poor and the commanding officer was tempted to break off the search, when *Alberni* near by got the same or another contact. *Kenogami* came up and also got an echo. The three ships began a deliberate attack and after another pattern of depth-charges had been dropped a great bubble of air rose to the surface of the water. Then came many bubbles, and then oil. It was no better than a "probable kill", but the convoy was moving ahead and the ships had to leave to rejoin it.

The rest of the day passed quietly, but as soon as darkness fell the attacks began again. The wolf-pack had been cruising at a distance and was moving in once more. Men who had had no sleep the night before and little through the day continued at action stations for another ten hours. The rattle of machine-gun fire and the boom of depth-charges went on all night, broken at times by the deeper roar of an exploding torpedo. This time, however, the fighting was not all in favour of the U-boats.

Two new corvettes, *Chambly* and *Moose Jaw*, had arrived in St. John's before the convoy set out. A few days after *Skeena* sailed with her escort group, *Chambly* and *Moose Jaw* had put to sea for training in the waters south of Greenland. They were now not far from the position in which SC-42 was under attack, and a signal from St. John's had reached them a few hours earlier. They were to sail to the convoy's assistance and their men were to get a chance very quickly to practise what they had learned.

The two ships neared the convoy in the dusk of early evening. Their first warning was the flare of two white rockets well down on the horizon, the signal that a ship had been torpedoed. *Chambly* increased her speed and made for the position with *Moose Jaw* keeping pace on her starboard side.

Seventeen minutes after the first rockets were sighted two more went up. A minute later *Chambly* got a submarine contact on her asdic. She followed the echo for two minutes, then let go her depth-charges. Just as she was getting ready to fire a second pattern a U-boat surfaced a mile away, about four hundred yards off *Moose Jaw*'s port bow. It swung quickly, streaming water from its tapered sides, and ran across the corvette's course. *Moose Jaw*'s gun-crew opened fire and the ship charged in to ram the U-boat, but suddenly the German's conning tower opened. Men began to climb out of it and the boat coasted to a stop.

Moose Jaw swung her bow away from the middle of the U-boat at which she had been aiming, and ran close alongside. Most of the Nazi crew were now standing by the conning tower with their hands in the air. As the two hulls touched, the U-boat's captain leaped from his own deck to the deck of the corvette, not even wetting his feet. Nothing like this had ever been heard of in the Canadians' training, and the ship backed off to prevent any further boarding. As it did so a few of the more stubborn Germans, still below at the U-boat's engines, got it under way again. *Moose Jaw* promptly surged forward and did what she had first intended. With a shattering crash her bow rammed into the U-boat's hull. The boat swung away with the impact and *Moose Jaw* plunged on for another two hundred yards. As she swung round some of the German crew, recovering their fighting spirit, made a rush for the gun forward on their deck. *Moose Jaw*'s gun spoke first and two or three shells screaming over the Nazis' heads soon put their hands in the air again.

By now *Chambly* had come up on the other side of the U-boat. Lieutenant Edward T. Simmons jumped to the deck with a boarding-party and ordered the Germans to climb back into the conning tower and lead the way below. They refused, and even the muzzles of pistols and submachine-guns could not make them change their minds. The U-boat had been scuttled; the sea-cocks had been opened and water was already flooding into her lower sections. The boarding-party nevertheless made a brave attempt to save her, for there was a great deal that was not yet known about German submarines and she would have been a valuable prize. They went down through the conning tower to

find that all instruments had been smashed, moved on to the generators and the lighting system which had also been put out of action. Then from beneath them came a warning rush of water and they turned back, but not quite soon enough.

With a sudden lurch the craft began to settle. As water came flooding in, stoker William I. Brown was sucked back into the swirl and drowned. The other men of the boarding-party tried to reach him but had to give up and scramble for safety themselves. They reached the deck, pushed their prisoners over the side ahead of them and swam for their ship. They had lost one man, and eleven Germans who had stood to their posts below went down with the boat.

The captain of the U-boat was a type rare in the underwater navy. When he was questioned in *Moose Jaw*'s wardroom, he claimed that he had given himself up in order to insist that the Canadians rescue his men. He got cold looks in reply and the flimsy explanation did not go down well even with his own crew. His chief quartermaster, the senior survivor after himself, refused to shake hands with him, and his men turned their backs when he tried to speak to them. His submarine, *U-501*, had come to grief on her first cruise, which was fair enough since few of the men in the two corvettes had more than a week at sea.

"Rejoined convoy" is the entry closing the incident in *Chambly*'s log, the diary in which ships record their daily doings. The battle was still flaring about SC-42. Two ships went down about nine in the evening. Shortly before one o'clock the next morning two more were sunk within five minutes of each other. There was no way in which the outnumbered escorts could screen the convoy completely. Whenever they moved to close a gap in the defences another gap was opened and an attacker thrust in. Morning brought relief again as the U-boats drew off, and at noon a welcome smudge appeared on the eastern horizon. The Newfoundland Escort Group had finished its mid-ocean task and the British escort force was arriving from Iceland. Fifteen ships had been sunk out of the sixty-four which set out and one more was to be lost before the convoy reached port.

All through the autumn of 1941 the savage battle continued. *Levis,* the first corvette to be lost, went down from a torpedo in September and she was soon to be followed by others. The toll of merchant vessels was staggering. Thousands of men and women, at work day and night in all the shipyards of Britain and Canada, could not make good the losses in that stormy ocean, crawling with a sinister enemy. For every merchant ship that was built, two were going down; and for every U-boat sunk the Germans were building ten.

Winter closed in and the convoys, still routed north around the tip of Greenland, made two-thirds of each voyage in icy arctic darkness. More and more corvettes were sailing with them now, always with more recruits fresh from the training-centres. The war demanded a lad long before he was ready. It used him hard, it taught him much, and it promised little. Many a man saw flaming ships go down on his first voyage. He saw the thick lake of oil, streaming from broken tanks, spread out on the water. He heard the cries of men in the midst of it, their throats choked with it, their hands and faces black. Sometimes he helped to drag a few on board, burned, wounded, retching, and exhausted. Often he watched helplessly as they fell behind the ship, tossed by the backwash, drifting away on the dark ocean. He looked ahead from his own deck and knew that if a torpedo struck, his chance of life was one in a hundred. The freezing cold of that black water washing along the side would kill him in five minutes. There were no special ships for rescue-work as yet, there were never enough boats and floats. Even a good life-jacket, equipped with lights and flares, was still a thing of the future.

As the little ships drove on, sleet and frozen spray covered them from stem to stern. Ice coated the guns a foot thick, caked on the depth-charges, rose in weird caverns climbing above the bridge. Waves washing along the decks froze into layer on layer of lumps and ridges, piling up on the weather side, tilting the ship and making it almost impossible to steer. One or two vessels turned over and sank from the sheer weight. Before an escort group was three days out of St. John's the bread in the ship's galleys became a mass of green mould. On the northward leg of the voyage, far up along the Greenland coast, fresh meat and vegetables spoiled as the battered refrigerators stopped working. With all the ice on each ship there was no place where it could be used to save the provisions of a hundred men. Hard biscuit and salt-beef, with lime-juice to stave off the spots and sores of scurvy, became the rations for Canadians in 1941 as they had been for Nelson's crews before them.

Unbathed, unshaven, freezing on their watches above decks and often soaking wet in their hours below, the men of the corvettes drove along through continual night. Gales hammered them, fog blinded them and arrows of driving sleet tore at their faces. The seas lifted in crested mountains and opened in great troughs; the ships riding them seemed to climb like goats and plunge like logs. Then, as the gales went down, came the long, thundering swells – the "milestones" – which struck the hulls with pile-driving force, knocking men from their feet or hurling them from their hammocks, breaking up the few hours of sleep.

There was always the danger of running out of fuel, for each voyage seemed to grow longer and harder. Time after time, struggling with gales and cross-seas which drove them far off their course or turning away on long zig-zags to avoid U-boats, captains found themselves nursing their last precious tons of oil. Sometimes, with tanks empty, they lay on the bleak sea waiting for a tow, sitting ducks for a U-boat and powerless to fight a storm.

Always among the crews there were desperately sea-sick lads who spent their hours off watch lying on lockers, in hammocks, at the foot of companion-ways or wherever they could find six feet of space. They were too sick to move, too sick to care whether they lived or died, but not quite sick enough to quit. They got no sympathy from their captains. Captains said that it was bad to sympathize with a sea-sick man. You left him to work out his fate. For some the fate was a shore job when the ships got home. But there were others – and more of them – who went whole voyages with hardly a morsel of solid food, who lived on soup and fruit-juice, did their work as long as they could stand or hold onto something, kept down their tortured innards and won the doubtful privilege of staying at sea.

The destroyers had been longer at war than the corvettes, and *Restigouche* as long as any. Suddenly, in the midst of that memorable winter, the prospect of a Christmas at home was dangled before her men. Now a salt-scarred veteran and "Rusty Guts" to all the navy, she had come with a convoy to Hvalfjord, Iceland, early in December. There she learned that she was to meet a west-bound convoy sailing from England and escort it to Halifax. On the afternoon of December 12, with five corvettes, she sailed to meet the convoy at a point south of Iceland.

The group came out of harbour into the teeth of a snowstorm driving on a full gale. Hours later, when the meeting-point was reached, the merchant ships were nowhere to be seen. *Restigouche*, faster than the corvettes, went on ahead to make a search. At dark, having found nothing, she came back to the other ships and the whole group moved along the course the convoy was supposed to take.

During the night and the early hours of the next morning the gale grew wilder. The ships struggled on through blinding sleet. About four o'clock in the afternoon a signal from the convoy reached *Restigouche* giving a position about thirty miles away. The ships steered for the new meeting-point, but before they had covered half of the thirty miles the gale had become a hurricane. Roaring seas lashed along the ships' decks, smashing up everything in their way. Walls of water climbed above the fo'c'sle-heads and arched in over the bridges. The sleet became a curtain of driving snow, shutting off the view completely. The escorts disappeared from each other's sight and not a ship of the convoy could be found.

The corvettes were forced to give up and ride with the wind. *Restigouche*, heading into the storm, found it almost impossible to steer, and half a dozen times great waves driving in from the side threatened to turn her over. At five o'clock on the afternoon of the second day there was a thunderous report high above the deck. The ship's foremast had cracked and a part of it came plunging down onto the forward funnel. With the mast went the ship's wireless, and there was nothing for it but to send up a party to rig a new aerial. Within half an hour men clinging to icy poles thirty feet above the deck had done the job and signals were coming through again from the Admiralty in London.

Meanwhile the towering seas were wrecking the quarter-deck. Depth-charges had broken loose and were charging back and forth with every roll of the ship. The hatch-covers which closed the companion-ways and shut off the lower decks had been ripped off and floods of water were washing below. The hatches had to be closed somehow and Sub-Lieutenant S. G. Moore fought his way aft toward them. He had just managed to get one of the covers in place when a great wave swept him back against the depth-charge rails, breaking his leg.

Other men took his place and the covers were secured at last. Then more trouble broke out at the forward end. Leaks opened in the sides and many sections were flooded as waves racked and pounded the ship. The cooking-fires in the galley went out, and only a small steam-jet rigged by the engineers made it possible to get a rare hot drink to the men. At four o'clock in the morning the steering-gear gave way and for an hour the destroyer lay helpless while it was being repaired.

The emergency steering-gear in the after part of the ship was already under six feet of water. At five o'clock a mightier blow from the sea knocked all the lighting system out of action. The battered vessel was thrown into total darkness while the fire-alarm, set off by the same blow, screamed eerily.

The storm continued without let-up for another day and a half. As it began to die down *Restigouche* received a signal telling her that the ships of the convoy she had set out to meet had been ordered to disperse and sail separately. She was relieved of her escort duties, but she had still to save herself. She had sprung a leak in her bottom and many sections of the ship were flooded to a depth of seven feet. Though the wind had gone down a little it was still blowing a full gale, and damaged as she was she could make no headway against it. She would have to turn back and she would turn with the weight of hundreds of tons of water heaving inside of her, dragging her over. If she were caught sidewise in a trough of the sea there would be no hope. She came about slowly, rolling sickeningly as the force of the storm struck her broadside on. Then she staggered erect, shedding water in floods as the turn was completed, and at last was running with the wind.

The problem now was to steer the ship with damaged gear and the wind and sea battering her from astern. There was no longer any hope of making Halifax, and she was in no condition to wait out the storm. She had been blown nearer to Scotland than to Iceland, and it was Scotland she decided to run for. Through the rest of the day and all through another night she staggered eastward with the whole ship's company working on repair- and bucket-parties.

There was serious danger of running out of fuel as salt water had leaked in and ruined the oil in two tanks. She was lop-sided from her flooded compartments and leaning heavily to port. All her pumps and all her bucket-men could not get the level of the flood below four feet. Officers and men, some wearing diving-masks to protect them from the fumes of calcium flares burning under water, were still hard at work on the afternoon of December 16 as *Restigouche* crawled slowly in through the harbour gate at Greenock.

Relatives in Halifax and in other homes across Canada would not see these men for Christmas, 1941. There was not a stitch of dry clothing on board the ship, nor a man who had had hot food or sleep in the past sixty hours. Nevertheless, from the wrong side of the Atlantic, the captain of *Restigouche* reported that "the decision to proceed to Greenock, as opposed to the long-hoped-for Christmas at home in Halifax, was accepted cheerfully. Every man, regardless of rank, rating, or branch, worked ceaselessly day and night for the good of the ship."

The raw Canadian youngsters were coming of age.

6. The St. Lawrence

THE United States was now our partner in the war, and this meant victory for the future. In the early months of 1942, however, it brought a swarm of U-boats to our very doorstep. Most of them came to attack the ships moving between American ports, but northwards along the Atlantic seaboard the wide mouth of our own St. Lawrence gaped invitingly. On the night of June 11 a torpedo drove home in the freighter *Nicoya* off the island of Anticosti. This was our first warning that a U-boat had invaded the Gulf, but our real trouble began with the arrival of Lieutenant-Commander Paul Hartwig in *U-517*.

Hartwig sailed from the German harbour of Kiel on August 8, 1942. He was a hard-drinking young man, but he was also a very fine U-boat officer, much admired by his crew. His first orders were to attack ships moving along the Labrador coast, and he reached the mouth of the Strait of Belle Isle on the morning of August 26. The Strait divides Labrador from Newfoundland, and it was a route for many convoys moving out of Sydney. The first appeared next morning and as it came in sight Hartwig fired two torpedoes and dived. A dull roar from above told him that one of his torpedoes had hit, and when he put up his periscope an hour or so later he saw the wreck of a large ship still blazing on the water. None of the escort ships had been able to locate him as he lay submerged, and the success encouraged him to push on down through the Strait.

Down this same strait Jacques Cartier had come four hundred years before, looking at the rocky shores on either hand and thinking them "the land that God gave Cain". Hartwig's feelings must have been very similar. In the afternoon he sighted another U-boat, U-165, riding low on the surface like himself. A friend was very welcome in this bleak stretch of hostile water, and the two boats closed for a talk. Just as they did so, however, the sound of aircraft engines came from above. A Canadian patrol plane was wheeling out in widening circles from the spot where the torpedoed ship had gone down in the morning. Both of the opened conning towers slammed shut before a word had been exchanged, there was a brief swirl on the water from two crash-dives and then nothing to be seen. Beneath the surface, however, the boats moved on in company and that night each got another ship.

They separated next day, for they knew that the escort forces of the Canadians would now be thoroughly aroused and it would be safer to travel alone. By the morning of August 29 Hartwig was well into the Gulf of St. Lawrence, and during the afternoon he came in sight of Anticosti Island. From there he began to patrol north-easterly and south-westerly, riding on the surface at night and travelling with his periscope just above water in day-time. The sweep continued, monotonous and tense, until the evening of September 2, when he saw ships approaching low on the horizon. He had been just surfacing in the gathering twilight and he remained on the surface as he began to shadow the convoy.

It was being escorted by the corvette *Weyburn* and one or two smaller ships, all we could yet spare from the battle in the Atlantic. As Hartwig moved in to attack, *Weyburn* caught sight of the glistening wash made by his conning tower. She fired rockets, got away two rounds from her forward gun, and bore down at full speed to ram. Hartwig waited coolly until *Weyburn* was within a thousand yards of him, then swung sharply, fired a torpedo past the corvette into the merchantman *Donald Stewart*, and dived.

As the flames from *Donald Stewart* lit up the sky *Weyburn* crossed the swirl of the U-boat's dive. Two depth-charges rolled from the rails at her stern but the rest of the pattern never got away. Her throwers had jammed at the moment of firing, and the two explosions astern of her were just enough to break up her asdic echo. She could not get back her contact in the seething water and after an hour's search she turned back to help the *Donald Stewart*. Hartwig and his men waited below, wondering at their freedom from attack, as the convoy swept away.

Next day Hartwig began to patrol between Anticosti Island and the Gaspé coast. Life was becoming dangerous now and there were many patrol planes overhead. One came screaming down out of a misty sky to drop a bomb squarely on the U-boat's deck. Hartwig's luck and nerve were still with him, however. The bomb failed to explode, and the captain and three of his men simply heaved it overboard.

By the night of September 6 Hartwig had worked his way up the river to within 250 miles of Quebec. Just before darkness fell he made out a line of ships coming toward him from the south-west. It was a convoy bound from Quebec to Sydney, escorted by the corvette *Arrowhead*, the armed yacht *Raccoon*, and three smaller vessels.

U-517 waited for full dark, coasting along at periscope depth four or five miles off from the ships as they drew abreast. Then she crept up to within a mile and sent a torpedo crashing into one of the merchantmen. She was a hundred feet down within five minutes, but this time *Arrowhead* was as quick and a full pattern of depth-charges came thundering after her. The double hull rang and shuddered, all the lights went out, and men were thrown about the cramped compartments in pitch blackness. They waited for a rush of water and were relieved when it did not come, but the sound of propellers could be heard through the hydrophone, the submarine's own listening device. The next thing might be the ping of the asdic against their hull, and Hartwig decided that it was time to play a new card. As *Arrowhead* groped above, searching for a death-grip, and the sound of her propellers grew louder, *U-517* released through a special vent a small, perforated metal cylinder about twice the size of a tomato-tin.

It was the *Pillenwerfer*, or submarine bubble-target, an ingenious decoy which was to cause the allied navies a great deal of trouble. A chemical in the tin, when mixed with the water outside, produced a cloud of bubbles which sounded to an operator exactly like the echo from asdic. *Arrowhead* picked up the false target. The ship changed course and followed a clear, apparently unmistakable echo which suddenly faded out as the decoy, having done its work, sank to the bottom. *Arrowhead* and the other escorts, mystified and disappointed, went back to help survivors from the torpedoed ship.

The rescue-work ended about midnight, and it was then noticed that *Raccoon* was missing. A few minutes later two heavy explosions were heard, several miles away. *Arrowhead* ran for the position but found no trace of *Raccoon* and the yacht was never seen again. She had probably been sunk by U-165 which was somewhere in the area, and several days later the body of one of her men was washed up on Anticosti Island.

The convoy went on, but the relentless Hartwig tackled it again shortly before daylight. This time he worked right in among the columns and fired three torpedoes at once, two from the tubes at his bow and one from astern. Each torpedo hit its mark, and the German was deep under water again as three ships burst into flames. *Arrowhead* was close on his track, but with blazing wrecks and drowning men all round her she could not make a proper search. Once again he made his escape.

Three days later Hartwig returned to the neighbourhood of Gaspé. The early morning of September 11 was dark, with a mist wreathing over the waters of the Gulf. The corvette *Charlottetown* and the minesweeper *Clayoquot* had delivered a convoy to Rimouski and were steaming back toward Gaspé, abreast of each other, about a mile apart and zig-zagging at fifteen knots. Their asdics failed them somehow in the choppy waters of the Gulf, and neither ship had any suspicion of the U-boat's presence until two torpedoes struck *Charlottetown* on the starboard side.

The corvette began to sink immediately and her men had just three minutes to get overboard before she disappeared. Not many of the crew had been hurt by the torpedoes, but as the stern of the ship went under a depth-charge exploded, killing six of the men in the water and injuring several others. There was the usual grim postponement of rescue-work while *Clayoquot* searched for the U-boat. She could find no echo and returned after an hour to take on board fifty-five survivors, many of them wounded.

During the following week four more ships went down, either from Hartwig's torpedoes or from the torpedoes of *U-165*. The two boats sometimes worked in company and sometimes alone. They glided through the Gulf and up the once-peaceful river, sinister grey shapes sometimes just breaking the surface, often far beneath. They seemed impossible to find until the glare of an explosion came, and even then they were too quick or skilful or lucky to be caught. The half-dozen corvettes and the few smaller ships which made up the escort force in the St. Lawrence had to grope among broken lines of merchantmen with the glow of fires lighting the darkness and the cries of desperate men coming to them from the pitchy waters. They sent their charges thundering down on every echo and possible echo, but never saw a conning tower heave to the surface or oil gush up from below. In the final battle of the week, however, they did manage to give *U-517* a fairly severe shaking. The gear for firing her torpedoes and the condenser for distilling fresh water from the sea were both damaged. Her men had to be rationed on water, they had to go without the beloved coffee which they usually drank in gallons, and they were no longer sure that they could hit what they aimed at.

In spite of it all Hartwig hung on for another three weeks. It was October 4 when he fired his last four torpedoes at the ships of a convoy moving down the river. All ran badly and missed, and it was time to go. The next day he nosed out of Cabot Strait and made for the open sea. He had sunk 31,000 tons of allied shipping, he had dodged twenty-seven bombs and he had had 118 depth-charges dropped too near him for comfort.

He was an enemy of great nerve and skill, and he would not be the last to appear in our home waters. The battle was no longer a remote tale echoing back from the mid-Atlantic. From the U-boat pens of Kiel and Wilhelmshaven and Saint-Nazaire and Lorient it had advanced to within two hundred miles of Quebec City.

7. "The End of the Beginning"

By the summer of 1942 there were thirteen destroyers, sixty-eight corvettes, twenty Bangor minesweepers and sixty smaller ships in the Canadian navy. Four "Tribals" – the new destroyers which were to be named after our Indian tribes – were building in our shipyards, along with forty-six corvettes and many lesser craft. Forty thousand men were on service, and the training-depots were now able to turn out ten thousand more each year.

The men and the ships already at sea were devoted almost entirely to the Atlantic battle. Few could be spared from it even for the defence of our own river. They were helping to hold the great life-line upon which everything depended; they were making it possible for sixty thousand tons of war supplies to move every day to the ports of the United Kingdom.

Every man in our ships had had much to learn, some of it grudgingly at first. The iron hand of naval discipline fell strangely on lads fresh from school or a job or a farm. Officers and officers' commands were sometimes tough to take. Petty officers and leading seamen, only a step above you in the ranks, were often the worst of all. You saw more of them, you were never out of their sight. They knew everything, and everything you did was wrong. They snapped at your heels, they routed you out of your mick, they made work for you and they made you do it over till it was right. There was never a minute, it seemed, when they were not hounding you through a drill, explaining, complaining, correcting, and starting again. Some day, thought many a man brooding alone on his first watches, he would find a way to get even. But the time never came.

Instead, and all too often, you found yourself suddenly in the midst of your first convoy battle. Everything was wild confusion, you had no idea of what was going on, yet somehow you were standing your post. You were doing things right, by instinct, without thinking, because you had been made to do them a hundred times over in the dismal routine of those drills. The familiar orders came, and they were welcome. The detested bark of the leading hand or the petty officer or the hard-boiled first lieutenant became the one friendly sound in the whole vast ocean and the flaming night. The man who knew what to do in those few terrible moments, the man whose voice had training and knowledge and assurance behind it, was a man you obeyed gladly. You might curse him again when the moment had passed, but you would not question his right to command. And if you looked at him afterward and knew you had done your job, and knew that he knew it, there was a bond formed that nothing could break.

There were thousands of such bonds now, and they were building the spirit and tradition of the navy. Each ship seemed to have a character of its own, each ship's company was a close-knit family, and the ships which worked together in the escort groups were larger families of families. *Skeena* and *Saguenay* had been the first to paint the funnels of their group in bands of red and white, forming the "Barber Pole" brigade. There were many other brigades now, wearing their distinctive marks, and each ship, of course, had acquired her nickname. *Restigouche* was "Rusty Guts", *Saint Laurent* was "Sally Rand", *Assiniboine* was "Bones"; and others were known with equal affection and disrespect in many harbours and over many thousand miles of sea.

Along with their nicknames most ships now wore their "badge", painted on the sides of the bridge or the gun-turret. It was the trade-mark and the boast, and it was strictly unofficial. The ship's company thought it up and it was worked out by the best artist on board, sometimes not very good. In *Calgary*'s badge a cowboy rode a bucking corvette, waving a six-shooter at a kneeling submarine. *Drumheller* had a flaming devil beating a tattoo on a drum. On *Galt*'s sides a grizzled old sailor, much resembling Popeye, spanked a U-boat across his knee, while *Moose Jaw* showed a fire-belching moose chasing a running Hitler.

The sheep-dog ships and the men who manned them had a right to their pride. They had a right to their fun, when they could get it. They had fought through thirty-five months of the war. They had endured, and they were growing stronger, and they felt a change in the world. Everywhere, on land and sea, an end was coming to the long story of defeat and disaster for the Allies. But still for many months yet the rhythm of the ocean convoys would be punctuated by the roar of torpedoes, the muffled thud of depth-charges and the bark and rattle of gun-fire.

Saint Croix, Skeena, and *Wetaskiwin* were the first ships to make their kills that summer. On July 24 *Saint Croix* was in mid-Atlantic with a convoy when, late in the afternoon, a look-out high up in the crow's-nest on her mast sighted a U-boat ten miles away. The German turned to run as the destroyer veered to chase him, and there was a race on the surface for the best part of an hour. Then, while still three miles ahead, the U-boat went under in a crash-dive. Her captain was probably quite satisfied with himself. He had led the Canadian far away from the convoy, and he was still well beyond asdic range.

Unhappily for him, *Saint Croix* guessed rightly as to the course he would take under water. She came over him, gained an asdic contact, and held on grimly. Two patterns of depth-charges brought no result at all. The third brought a little oil seeping to the surface, but this was not much encouragement for the men in the destroyer. U-boat captains still sent oil bubbling up through their torpedo-tubes, hoping to convince an attacking ship that they had sunk. The echo began to grow fainter, which could mean that the submarine was going down hurt but could also mean that she was getting away. The fourth pattern of depth-charges settled the question. Over the place of the explosion, gathering slowly from the depths, rose a nasty, oily litter of clothing, pocket-books, German cigarettes and packages of German food. The men who had owned them would not need them again. Two hundred feet below, the U-boat had cracked open and was settling to the sea-floor.

Skeena's and *Wetaskiwin's* kill came ten days later, seven hundred miles to the east of Newfoundland. It began with a doubtful asdic echo, and the two ships never saw their victim. For five hours they combed back and forth over miles of sea, hammering with depth-charges as they grew more certain of the contact. At last their grisly evidence rose to the surface, while gulls wheeled down to the water between the two ships. "Plenty of wreckage over this way," signalled *Wetaskiwin*. "I am lowering a whaler to pick up the guts," was *Skeena's* reply.

Skeena and *Wetaskiwin* had knocked out one of the members of a wolf-pack which was assembling round their convoy. *Sackville*, another of the corvettes in escort, was soon to have her turn. Just at dark next evening she sighted a U-boat on the surface and raced after it into the gathering gloom. Behind her the brilliant white light of "snow-flake" flares lifted above the convoy. It meant a torpedoing, and she wheeled back. As she did so the low silhouette of a second U-boat appeared between her and the merchant ships. Before she could reach him he was in among the columns of the convoy and out the other side.

Sackville had to let him go and take up station again on her own side of the convoy. She had hardly done so when another merchantman blew up, spewing out flame and wreckage and lighting the sea with an evil glare. *Sackville* had a brief glimpse of the attacker, speeding away on the surface with the gloomy, fog-ridden night closing about him. She put up a star-shell as she turned in pursuit and the light came just in time to show the enemy's bow tilting forward in a dive. *Sackville* rode into the swirl of the dive and her first depth-charge brought the U-boat's bow leaping from the water. The glistening, shadowy hull lifted at a sharp angle, revealing nearly sixty feet of its length. Then, as the explosions of other charges mushroomed about it, it slipped back and disappeared. *Sackville* came in over the spot again and dropped ten more charges. There was a huge explosion under the water and oil came flooding to the surface. It was more than probably a kill, but there was no time to make sure. The corvette turned back for the convoy.

She was hardly in station again when she heard the sound of propellers, very near in the fog. A U-boat, just two hundred yards ahead, was running across her bows. *Sackville* went full speed to ram, and as she did so the German turned back and ran straight in on her. He was trying to get inside her turning circle, so close that the muzzle of her four-inch gun could not be brought down to bear on him.

Sackville spun round onto the German's course and the two craft ran zig-zagging through the foggy blackness, *Sackville* attempting to ram, the U-boat swerving to avoid. They swung apart for an instant, the corvette's gun was brought to bear, and a four-inch shell caught the German squarely at the base of the conning tower. Bursts from *Sackville's* machine-guns rattled into the conning tower at point-blank range, and then bounced off a closed hatch as the U-boat went into a crash-dive. It was the end of a busy night's work for *Sackville* and a "probably damaged" added to her other score.

Assiniboine's turn came just five days later. She was four hundred miles off Newfoundland with a convoy when late in the afternoon a besetting fog lifted for a moment to reveal a U-boat six miles away. The destroyer gave chase, and though the fog soon closed round the German, he was not as safe as he thought. The beam of the destroyer's new radar equipment was now reaching out across the surface of the water to find him. Radio waves which he could not detect and as yet knew nothing about were striking his hull and sending back their echo. On the running green ribbon of the plot in *Assiniboine*'s radar-room the echoes were appearing as a series of dots or "blips", each one of which showed his position as he moved. He was in the grip of another of the great secret weapons designed by British and Canadian scientists. It had already helped to win the battle of Britain in the air. Now it was coming to the ships at sea.

Like asdic in the beginning, it still had its faults, and two or three times in the next hour the German seemed to be lost. Each time, however, the fog lifted for a moment and showed him still weaving away. He must have been mystified by the way the Canadian clung to him, but he still showed no intention of diving. Instead, as *Assiniboine* came in with the bow wave climbing high over her fo'c'sle, he let go a hail of fire and ran straight for her. He was making for the charmed circle where the destroyer's guns would not bear and she would be unable to ram. *Assiniboine* swung away as she saw his intention, the German swung with her, and for thirty-five minutes the two craft ran weaving and dodging together, blasting at each other with every gun they had.

They were so near that the men in *Assiniboine* could see the U-boat captain standing in his conning tower and bending down to pass wheel-orders. Most of the time the range was too close to get the four-inch guns to bear, but every machine-gun, rifle, and pistol in the ship was in action. "We threw everything but the potato-masher at him," said one

man later. *Assiniboine* was taking her punishment in return.
The German's gun-fire riddled the woodwork of the bridge
around the captain. Fires licked along by the wheel-house
and then began to break out in other parts of the ship.
Machine-gun bullets and incendiaries from the U-boat's
forty-millimetre cannon swept along the deck wounding
several men. The youngest lad on board, Ordinary Seaman

Kenneth Watson, was killed as he ran for a gun with a shell in his arms.

For an instant one of the destroyer's guns came fully to bear. A shell screamed out and men in *Assiniboine* saw the German captain go down as a hole gaped in his conning tower. He was killed instantly, as they learned afterward. Some of the U-boat's crew now tried a rush forward to their own main gun, but they were blasted into the water by *Assiniboine*'s machine-gun fire. Three or four times the swerving U-boat had avoided the destroyer's attempts to ram. Now, with another man in command, she attempted to dive, holding a steady course for a minute or so. In that time, just as her bow was tilting down, *Assiniboine*'s bow crashed into her. It was a glancing blow which sent the destroyer swerving away. As she turned back to ram again the submarine's bow lifted from the water and her stern began to settle. She was heavily damaged but still making about ten knots and still firing. *Assiniboine* rammed again, and as she passed heaved over a pattern of shallow-set depth-charges which bounced the German clear out of the water. Then came a shell from one of the destroyer's after guns, opening a great gash in the bow. The U-boat pitched forward and sank while a yell rose from *Assiniboine* "which must have frightened U-boats for ten miles around us".

Still the story of the summer was not complete. There were American planes over some of the convoys now, and on August 28 the corvette *Oakville* was led by one of them to the spot where she had bombed a U-boat and driven it under. *Oakville* blew the boat to the surface, swept the deck with her gun-fire, rammed, and then for good measure heaved a depth-charge under the German's stern. Her boarding-party was onto the deck in minutes and promptly shot the only two men who tried to make a fight of it. The rest of the crew piled quickly and meekly out of their sinking boat. The underwater navy was now faced by some tough ships and men.

In the autumn of 1942 seventeen Canadian corvettes were withdrawn from the Atlantic to sail with a great allied expedition for the conquest of North Africa and the Mediterranean. By the first months of 1943 the turn of the war had come. The Germans were beaten in North Africa, Italy was on the brink of invasion, the Mediterranean was an allied lake. Our ships had done their bit in making it so; *Ville de Quebec, Port Arthur,* and *Regina* had each got a submarine. But if there was a new confidence in the men who sailed the ships, there was no elation yet. *Louisbourg* and *Weyburn* had been lost in the Mediterranean and the fifteen remaining corvettes were all back in the Atlantic. The convoys were still being harried and torn by an enemy who would never give up. The veteran *Ottawa,* sunk by a torpedo in September, had been added to our own toll of ships. The endless battle went on and there would still be bitter losses in the midst of those gale-ridden wastes.

8. *"The Beginning of the End"*

THROUGH January, February, and March of 1943 some of the largest wolf-packs of the war crept out from German harbours and from their bases at Saint-Nazaire and Lorient along the Bay of Biscay. By the beginning of March seventy U-boats were on station in the north-west Atlantic, cutting across the convoy routes in three great lines of patrol. There were other groups behind them nearer to the United Kingdom, there were U-boats far to the south in the Caribbean, and there were still other packs in the northern seas along the supply routes to Russia. They were met now by more and better escort ships and by skilful, battle-hardened men, yet in the four great convoy battles of March thirty-seven allied merchant vessels were sent to the bottom.

Early in April the U-boats, still increasing in numbers, began to close in on the western side of the Atlantic. They were pressing for a decision, desperately, for they seemed to sense that their time was short. Behind the battle at sea another battle was going on. It was being fought out in shipyards, in laboratories, in aircraft factories, and on landing-fields, and it was clear now that the side which won it would also win the battle of the Atlantic.

The escort ships, always held close to the convoys by the need to protect their merchantmen, could seldom pursue and hunt down a running U-boat. There was a need for other groups of ships which would sail as hunters only. There was a need for air cover and air patrol, for planes could cover a great area and find a U-boat quicker than any ship. There was a need for new weapons, for every U-boat which came down a German slipway seemed to be better equipped and more dangerous than the last.

The allied hunting groups were being formed. Fast destroyers, and the new frigates which were almost as large as destroyers, were arming and training. Small aircraft-carriers were being made ready to sail with them, each carrying six planes armed with radar, asdic, guns, and depth-charges. Great long-range patrol planes – the new "Liberators" – would soon be flying from bases in Newfoundland, Greenland, Iceland, and the United Kingdom. Their wide-sweeping arcs would intersect far out over the middle Atlantic; there would soon be no more of the "black pits" where U-boats were safe from the air and the escorts fought them blind.

Yet all this the Germans knew, and all this they were preparing to meet. Their shipyards, laboratories, and aircraft factories were busy too, and their undersea navy seemed almost on the edge of victory in the late days of March. The

allied escort forces had never been so hard-pressed. It seemed
that all their reinforcements and all the skill and knowledge
gained in four years of war would not be enough to defeat
the growing fury of the wolf-packs. The last of the winter
storms roared across the seas, ships of the convoys still
plunged to the bottom gashed by torpedoes, and the sleek
grey shapes of the attackers seemed everywhere about them.
The race was a race on land, on sea, and in the air now, and
the result was still in doubt.

Early in April five British hunting groups set sail within a
few days of each other. About the same time clearing skies
began to release the new Liberators, which had been held
to their landing-fields by foul weather. For a few weeks the
convoys crawling over the vast wastes of sea saw little change,
but the change had come. On April 25, three hundred miles
south-east of Greenland, a convoy was moving into the zone
of a gathering wolf-pack. The day before it had seen an
unfamiliar plane, very large and wearing the roundels of the
Royal Canadian Air Force, circling in the distance and
wheeling away. Now, about mid-morning, the funnels of six
friendly warships heaved over the horizon. They were the
ships of a hunting group, summoned by the Liberator, and
in the midst of them was the squat shape of the aircraft-
carrier *Biter*. Six planes shot up from *Biter's* deck as the
group approached, and swung out in wide arcs over the sea.
The convoy did not see a conning tower or feel a torpedo
for the rest of that voyage. Within an hour one of the planes
had pinned down a U-boat and a warship had charged up to
destroy it. The rest of the pack had been driven under and
dispersed.

The same thing began to happen elsewhere over the Atlantic in the weeks that followed. Early in May *Chambly* and *Drumheller* had a closer glimpse of the changing battle. Far ahead of their convoy, on May 12, the signal came that a Liberator had sunk a U-boat which was moving in to attack. Two days later other Liberators sank one and attacked five more, breaking up the pack before it could come in range of the convoy. A night later, just before dusk, *Chambly* sighted a lone U-boat on the horizon and gave chase. The submarine was quite as fast as the corvette and in the old days would probably have escaped. This time a plane from *Biter* took off, attacked the U-boat with depth-charges, and circled the area of its dive until *Chambly* came up. Hard on her heels came the ships of the hunting group, and sixteen seconds after their attack a mass of oily wreckage gushed to the surface.

It was not depth-charges which had gone down this time. Instead, the lead ship of the hunting group had moved in with an odd-looking battery of twenty-four spigotted heads pointing from her forward deck. The new weapon had something of the spiky appearance of a hedgehog, and "hedgehog" it was named. As it fired, twenty-four bombs carrying a new and powerful explosive had leaped from the short barrels which held them and shot out over the water. They had plunged in a neat circle about 250 yards ahead of the ship's bow, and as one of them went down it had touched the U-boat's hull and blown it to pieces.

Only the bomb which touched the U-boat had been set off. It had been found that depth-charges, which exploded whether or not they were within range, often broke up the asdic echo and let an enemy get away. Hedgehog would fire only on contact, only if a kill were certain. The asdic echo, once gained, could be firmly held in undisturbed water, while the bombs went down in wide circles of death to find their mark.

Drumheller's glimpse of the new day came twenty-four hours later, with the same convoy. Far beyond her horizon a plane from *Biter* had attacked a U-boat which was fighting back on the surface. A British patrol plane, sweeping far out from its base in Iceland, sighted the battle, signalled *Drumheller*, and led her to the spot. The U-boat dived as the corvette appeared, and *Drumheller* moved in over the swirl and dropped depth-charges. Then came the British frigate *Lagan* from the hunting group, and *Drumheller* stood aside while the hedgehog attack began. The bombs fell, circling the target-area. There were a few seconds of tense waiting and then a rumbling explosion far beneath. The sea's heaving blackness churned white and green. Oil followed, and then a litter of wreckage amid which there rose a huge bubble of air sixty feet tall from the U-boat's shattered pressure-tanks. It had been sent to the bottom by the four allied arms which now protected the convoys: shore-based patrol planes, carrier planes, ships of the close escort, and ships of the hunting groups.

Everywhere over the Atlantic the story was the same. By the end of May it was clear that defeat was looming for the U-boats. They still fought hard and took instant advantage of any chance which opened. With one convoy, in a wild week when gales grounded patrol planes and held the carrier planes to their decks, twelve ships out of forty-three were torpedoed. Yet, against that, thirty-seven U-boats were sunk and thirty-two were damaged. At long last the German undersea craft were being destroyed faster than they were coming into service.

They drew back to their bases in June and returned in July bristling with heavy anti-aircraft guns. The attempt to fight it out on the surface with planes was a failure; forty-six U-boats went to the bottom in that month. For a time they were practically driven from the Atlantic and allied hunting groups went after them into the Bay of Biscay, savagely attacking them as they limped home or catching them as they put out from their bases. We were on the offensive in the sea warfare now and victory was in the air. But we were not finished with the Germans yet.

One of the support groups in the Bay of Biscay was made up of the British frigates *Nene* and *Tweed* and the Canadian corvettes *Edmundston, Calgary,* and *Snowberry.* In the early afternoon of August 25 an American Liberator passed over them and signalled: "Twenty-one enemy planes heading this way." Twelve minutes later fourteen slender-bodied German Dorniers and seven JU-88 dive-bombers flying at a height of 4,000 feet appeared ahead of the ships. The JU-88's seemed to be acting as escorts and the Dorniers, which were patrol bombers, were not behaving in their usual way. They swung far out to starboard of the convoy, and for a few minutes ran on a course parallel with the ships. Then they suddenly turned in, bore down on their targets, and from beneath the body of each plane a small, winged glider shot forward about 200 feet, leaving a trail of white vapour.

As the barrage from the ships' guns speckled the sky, the

gliders banked over and shot downward at a speed of nearly 400 miles an hour. They were controlled from the Dorniers above, and they seemed to be speeding relentlessly for the ships. Allied seamen were getting their first look at the German glider-bomb, the "Chase Me Charley", as a British yeoman of signals nicknamed it that afternoon.

The ships were racing at full speed, ducking and weaving to avoid the bombs. Luckily for them, the German pilots had not had much practice and were not very good with them yet. The bombs exploded in the water, harmlessly but much too near for comfort. The senior frigate *Nene*, zigzagging wildly, signalled *Snowberry*, "What is your best speed?"

"Fifteen knots," was the answer, drawing the retort from *Nene*, "Don't give us that; we're doing eighteen and we can't shake you." *Snowberry*'s engineer officer later admitted that he had thought a special effort was called for and had "coaxed ten more revolutions out of the old ice-cream freezer".

The new weapon failed in its first attempt, but two days later it nearly cost us our first Tribal-class destroyer, *Athabaskan*. Twenty Dorniers came in on her group through a heavy barrage and released their bombs more accurately than before. One of them was dead on line for *Athabaskan* all the way. It struck the destroyer with shattering impact, passed clean through the hull below the bridge, and exploded when it was six feet clear of the other side. *Athabaskan* was hidden from the other ships in a great pall of steam and smoke. Her fore part was wrecked, five of her men were killed and twelve wounded. She was heavily afire and her forward guns were knocked out. Nevertheless, her after guns remained

steadily in action and when the attack ended she was got under way again. She made Plymouth safely after a dangerous four-day voyage, but she was a crippled ship which would not see action again for many months.

Nor was the glider-bomb the only weapon with which the Germans fought back. On September 19 a newly-formed hunting group consisting of the Canadian destroyers *Saint Croix* and *Saint Francis*, the Canadian corvettes *Chambly*, *Sackville*, and *Morden*, and the British frigate *Itchen*, was ordered to reinforce the escort for Convoy ONS-202. The convoy was sailing west from the United Kingdom, and the air about it was once more full of U-boat signals. It seemed that after nearly two months of quiet along the convoy routes, a new attack was preparing. Nothing had happened by the time the hunting group arrived, but the next night, well astern of the convoy, there was hot and disturbing action.

The British frigate *Lagan*, one of the ships in close escort, had detected a surfaced U-boat and had pursued it. The German had run well back from the convoy and dived as *Lagan* drew near him. She had moved in to make a hedgehog attack. Just as she did so, a torpedo which could not have come from the same U-boat had taken her in the stern and blown away thirty feet of her length.

When the report came to *Saint Croix* she turned back to investigate. She found *Lagan* settling in the water and began an asdic search about her. Suddenly, and without any warning, she was hit by a torpedo dead astern, then by a second. She began to lean toward the water, heavily wounded, making preparations to abandon ship. To *Itchen*, a few miles away, she signalled, "Am leaving the office." It was the last word from *Saint Croix*. Just as the signal left her lamp, she was hit by a third torpedo and was gone in three minutes.

It was *Itchen's* responsibility to search for the enemy before rescuing the survivors of *Saint Croix*. She signalled *Polyanthus*, another ship of the escort, to come to their help and herself disappeared on the hunt. *Polyanthus* never arrived. On the way to the scene she was torpedoed astern and sank. Only one survivor was picked up by *Itchen* next day. *Saint Croix's* men were in the water for thirteen freezing hours before *Itchen* got back to take eighty-one of them on board.

It seemed that night that the black times on the Atlantic had returned. Uneasiness grew the next day as the captains of the warships traded their signals. Three ships had been torpedoed, and all by torpedoes which struck them astern in the region of the propellers. This was unusual, since a ship "beam-on", or sidewise, offered a better target. It also seemed that each ship had been decoyed into position by one U-boat for attack by a second.

The rumour of a new weapon, an acoustic torpedo "homed" or guided to the ship by the sound of its propellers, had been going round the ports for several months. It was clear now that the rumour was, for once, correct. *Lagan*, *Saint Croix*, and *Polyanthus* had been led by a surfaced U-boat toward the position of the attacking boat which was lying submerged. The torpedoes which hit them had probably been fired from beam on, but they had been under the guidance of a new device which swung them round in a wide arc and homed them in on the sound of the propeller-wash.

There were nine attacks on the convoy during the next night, and though they were fought off without loss there had been much of the old dash and confidence in the U-boats methods. Fog prevented much action on the following day, but at 9.30 that evening, as the fog cleared away, the attacks began again. *Morden*, running out ahead of the convoy, sighted a surfaced U-boat and lit it up with star-shell. A number of escorts came surging after her and there was a confused flurry of gun-fire.

Itchen ran out ahead of them all, and switched on her searchlight. The U-boat rode on the water three or four hundred yards ahead of her. Men in the other ships heard a burst from *Itchen's* guns and then her searchlight went out. There was a second of darkness, then "a tremendous, orange-coloured mushroom of flame and an ear-shocking explosion". *Itchen* vanished from the sea, and of all those on board her only the lone survivor from *Polyanthus*, one man from *Saint Croix*, and one man from *Itchen* herself were saved.

The convoy proceeded sombrely to port, with total losses of four warships and seven merchantmen. The German radio was trumpeting enormous claims for its new, invincible torpedo. It was a deadly weapon and it would cost us many ships, yet already the plans to meet it were well advanced. Within two weeks ships were streaming "foxers" astern, long cables with metal noise-makers on the end. The noise-makers made a sound like propellers, drew the torpedoes to themselves, and exploded them at a safe distance. Allied weapons and defences were now abreast or ahead of anything the Germans could devise, and no one weapon could turn back the tide of ships. It was flooding eastward across an ocean securely held and it was closing in on the gates of Fortress Europe.

9. Gathering of the Giants

In May of 1945 a Russian war correspondent entering Berlin and looking at the ruins about him wrote with something like awe, "It is as if giants with colossal hammers had beaten Hitler's city into the earth." Giants indeed they were, and as the autumn of 1943 wore away into the spring of 1944 the last gathering of their strength began. Far in the east Russia was making ready for her great attacks across the plains of Europe. Over the western ocean came the thousands of ships and landing-craft, the hundreds of thousands of men, the cargoes of tanks and guns and shells which would be assembled in the ports of England and launched across the Channel onto the shores of France.

One hundred and ten ships and ten thousand men of Canada were to be a part of the great invasion force. Some of them were still on the North Atlantic as 1944 began, for Canadians did most of the escort work now around convoys which often numbered as many as 150 vessels. Others of our ships were already in British waters, training and making ready for D-Day, the day of invasion. And still others were at work in a new kind of war, for not only the U-boats but the German surface ships must now be swept from the seas.

When invasion came it would thrust directly across the Channel from the south coast of England to Baie de la Seine on the coast of France. It would cut through the great mine-field, the barrier of underwater bombs held in place below the surface by long wires and weights, which the Germans had strung along their coast. It would be powerful enough to sweep aside any German ships which came out to meet it. But it was not likely that the Germans would make that attempt. It was more probable that they would drive in on the flanks of the great expedition, and the likeliest direction was from the Bay of Biscay. In these waters, lying southward from the English Channel and washing the western coast of France, the Germans still had many ships and here they must be found and destroyed.

In this work our Tribal-class destroyers were now coming into their own. *Athabaskan* was a sound ship again. *Iroquois* had gone to sea ahead of her, and *Haida, Huron, Algonquin,* and *Sioux* had followed. They were far more powerful ships than any we had ever known, and far more wonderfully equipped. They each carried a crew of 250 men. They could reach speeds of thirty-five knots. They had every latest improvement in asdic and anti-submarine weapons. They carried tubes for launching torpedoes and bristled with anti-aircraft cannon and machine-guns. Each had six main guns mounted in turrets, three forward and three aft, and each gun could fire a heavy shell with deadly accuracy at a range of ten miles. Nor did darkness and fog any longer prevent the ranging of the guns. Radar, wonderfully improved since its first beginnings, was now used to control the gunnery. Men at lighted plotting-tables could sit shut away from the deck and the sea, tracking an enemy by the "blips" of his silhouette on the radar dial. They could pass his position to the gunners, the hair-line dials of the gun-sights would follow the radar reports, and the instant they came "on target" a shell would hurtle through the gloom, plunging for the unseen hull.

War was becoming a thing of deadly automatons, still controlled by men. The sailors in the Tribals were no longer the green lads who had gone to sea four years before. They had done their time in the other destroyers and in the corvettes and lesser craft. They had come along step by step to master the ways of the sea. Now they had mastered the new and terrible instruments which had been placed in their hands. They knew them and they had confidence in them, but they also knew war and their enemy. Nothing was sure in war, nothing could remove the risks and the chances of failure. Radar was no secret to the Germans now. They also had good ships and marvellous equipment. The men of the German surface navy, though they had been battered and shamed by the greater ships of the Royal Navy, were still of the same calibre as the men in the U-boats. If they were desperate now as they saw the tide of the war turning against them, they would be all the more dangerous because of it.

In April of 1944 we had clear proof both of the powers of our own ships and the powers of the enemy. At two o'clock on the morning of April 26, *Haida, Huron,* and *Athabaskan* were sweeping down through the Bay of Biscay. They were in company with the British cruiser *Black Prince* and the British destroyer *Ashanti,* and they were on the look-out for German destroyers. At a few minutes after two, radar echoes began to come in and the warships followed. At nineteen minutes after two *Black Prince* fired star-shell and revealed three German "Elbings" at a range of eight miles.

The Elbings were small, fast destroyers. As the star-shell burst over them they turned away and began to feed out a smoke-screen. *Haida, Huron, Athabaskan,* and *Ashanti* raced after them with their guns blazing and shells from the Germans splashing about them in the water. Soon they were running blind through clouds of wreathing, greyish-white smoke, fitfully lighted as *Black Prince* put up more star-shell.

Ashanti scored the first hit at thirty-one minutes after two. Five minutes later another bright red flash spumed up through the smoke, though it was impossible to tell which destroyer had scored. By 3.20 the flying Elbings, occasionally running out of their smoke-screen, were hugging the French coast. *Haida* noticed, as the smoke closed down again, that her three radar contacts had decreased to two, indicating that one German had fanned out from the others.

Five minutes later she caught sight of him. He was two and a half miles to starboard and was making off to the south and west. With *Athabaskan* following, *Haida* turned at right-angles and sent a salvo of three shells crashing onto the Elbing's deck. Her second and third salvoes struck squarely amidships, starting great fires, and after them more shells came raining down from *Athabaskan.* At twenty-one minutes after four *Haida* reported to *Black Prince*, "Enemy has sunk."

Two days later, on April 28, *Haida* and *Athabaskan* sailed on another patrol. Their first contact came at one minute to four in the morning. *Athabaskan* reported an echo to port at a range of fourteen miles, and *Haida* immediately picked up the same echo. At first there seemed to be two ships, then came a series of "blips" which indicated a third and smaller vessel.

The range closed to five miles and at 4.12 *Athabaskan* fired star-shell. Two destroyers, both Elbings, stood out in the orange-pink glow of the bursts. As a smoke-screen billowed about the Germans, *Haida* and *Athabaskan* opened fire and with the first roar of their guns turned their bows directly toward the enemy. It was done to give the narrowest possible target for torpedoes from the German destroyers, but this time it was too late for there was another enemy.

Athabaskan had barely steadied on her new course when a huge sheet of flame shot from her after part into the early-morning darkness. She had been hit by a torpedo from an Elbing or from the third smaller vessel which was never sighted. She slowed down, turned slowly to port, and stopped. The propellers at her stern had been smashed and her rudder broken.

Large fires broke out above and below decks, both in the after part and amidships. All after guns were knocked out immediately and in a moment or two fire from the forward guns also ceased. As the stern began to settle the order "Stand by to abandon" was given. Boats were made ready but they were not lowered as there seemed to be some hope of saving the ship. Hands began to prepare cables for towing. The destroyer was fiercely aflame, but a fire-party managed to get a pump aft where the blaze was worst. Just as they were getting it into action, however, the tons of shells and explosives in the magazine blew up. A column of flame and smoke towered in the sky and was seen by ships thirty miles away.

With the second explosion the ship gave a tremendous heave to starboard, swung back slowly onto an even keel and then listed to port. The men who were still on board and alive and conscious managed to shove a few carley floats overside and follow them into the water. They had a minute or so to push themselves away from the writhing steel sides above them. Then the blazing wreck up-ended slowly in the water and slid under amid clouds of steam and the roar of escaping air. On the oily, heaving blackness of the sea there remained only a few bobbing lights attached to the life-jackets of *Athabaskan's* survivors who were floating, many of them barely conscious, within five miles of the German-held coast.

For *Haida* the grim duty of seeking out the enemy came first. When the torpedo struck *Athabaskan* she had run across in front of her sister ship to lay a smoke-screen. Then she had turned away at full speed and resumed her pursuit of the Elbings. She had already hit one of them and, just at the moment when *Athabaskan* blew up five miles astern, another of her salvoes landed squarely on the deck of the same ship. The German, hopelessly damaged, ran in for the coast and grounded himself. He still continued to fire, however, and *Haida*, coming in as close to the rocks as she dared, poured salvo after salvo into him. The flames mounted above his guns at last and the guns fell silent. With dawn breaking and the other Elbing beyond her reach, *Haida* turned back to do what she could for the men of *Athabaskan*.

As she reached their position *Haida* was five miles off the French coast, within range of shore batteries and liable to air attack at any minute. She stopped and put down all her boats and floats. Scramble-nets were lowered over the side and word was passed from the bridge that the ship would remain for fifteen minutes. Her own men went down the scramble-nets to drag up dazed and exhausted survivors. Her motor launch also went over the side, manned by a party of three volunteers in charge of Leading Seaman W. A. MacLure.

Haida remained stopped for fifteen minutes and in that time thirty-eight men were rescued. After that, as day broadened, she could stay no longer. The first responsibility of her captain was to see to the safety of his ship. Word was passed along that *Haida* would go ahead in five minutes. The warning was repeated at one-minute intervals as rescue-parties still combed the sea. Sixty seconds after the last warning the order "slow ahead" was given.

The water began to boil back along the destroyer's sides. She moved past little clusters of men floating in life-jackets or clinging to wreckage. Hands clutching at her scramble-nets lost their grip. Two of her own crew who had gone down the nets were washed off by the back-rush and remained in the water with the survivors they had not been able to reach. Then, as *Haida* grew small in the distance, three German minesweepers put out from the coast to make prisoners of the men who were left.

MacLure and the three men in *Haida*'s motor launch had been left behind and they now had eight men in their boat, including the two shipmates who had been washed from the scramble-nets. They were not going to be captured if they could help it, and when the minesweepers appeared they set off in the direction of England. One of the German ships chased them briefly and then turned away. With no enemy at their heels, but with a very balky engine, they began the cross-channel voyage.

The best they could get out of their craft was a tiresome three knots. In mid-afternoon a flight of allied bombers passed over from the direction of England, but did not see them. An hour or so later came three planes which they took to be Spitfires, flying very low. As they stood up, shouting and waving their hands, the aircraft roared in at a height of about twelve feet, then zoomed upward to show the black crosses of the *Luftwaffe* on the under side of their wings. In the early evening two more planes appeared and were eyed with great suspicion. This time, however, there was no mistake. The planes were British fighters and they signalled an acknowledgment as flags from the launch spelled out *"Athabaskan, Canada, Navy"*. Three more planes followed them and wheeled overhead until a rescue craft of the Royal Air Force came charging out from the coast. By midnight the men from the launch were in hospital in England, bringing the total of *Athabaskan's* survivors to forty-four. The captain and 128 of the ship's company had been lost and eighty-three were prisoners of war.

Through the last days of April and on into May the destroyer sweeps continued in the Bay of Biscay. Other ships were combing the English Channel and the North Sea, clearing the invasion route and the waters to either side of it. Thousands of vessels crowded the English harbours or moved from port to port around the coast. Many of our own ships were among them. We now had two flotillas of small, fast motor-torpedo-boats working with English boats in the Channel. Nearly all our destroyers and eleven of our new frigates were on patrol with British squadrons. *Prince Henry* and *Prince David* had arrived, now converted into landing-ships. Like the hundreds of other landing-ships, they would carry flotillas of small, flat-bottomed, motor-driven assault-craft to stations within a few miles of the French coast. Then the craft would be lowered to the water, crowded with the first wave of the shock-troops, and would go in on their own. There were two Canadian flotillas of larger landing-craft which would cross the Channel under their own power. Nineteen of our corvettes were making their last preparations or were already escorting groups of invasion craft to the points from which they would sail.

May ended and the restless movements of the ships continued. The men on their decks saw the great camps of the armies on shore. They saw troop-transports already crowded, and long lines of freighters swinging at anchor. They saw masses of guns, tanks, trucks, and strange vehicles they could not name piled up on decks or crowded on wharves, waiting. They themselves waited, or sailed on patrol, or crawled with convoys from port to port. Everywhere they felt the great tensing, the great gathering. But no one knew when D-Day would come. No one knew when the next curt sailing order would take him to the coast of France.

On June 5 the order came. At twelve o'clock in the morning seven Canadian landing-craft slipped their lines from Southampton dock and joined a line of similar craft threading its way out of the crowded anchorage. Two hours astern of them in the great stream came nineteen more Canadian landing-craft. *Algonquin* moved out with British destroyers of the bombardment force at 6.15 in the evening, *Prince Henry* and *Prince David* got under way at 9.00, and *Sioux* followed at 10.45.

From many ports now, all round the English coast, thousands of ships were moving to the assembly point. On the maps in the secret war-rooms it had been a circle ten miles in diameter just south of the Isle of Wight. By the early evening of June 5, 1944, it was a stretch of heaving sea churned by innumerable propellers. Warships, troop-transports, merchantmen, and weirdly assorted special craft of every size and kind were arranging themselves in groups, each group scheduled for a certain position off the beaches at a certain time. As they formed they began to look like individual convoys, each separated by exact intervals. Warships moved ahead, escorts took station around the groups of transports and freighters, landing-craft crawled away in long strings. The whole mass of shipping began to feed out of the assembly area in ten great streams. With each stream separated from the next by an interval of two miles, it flowed southward toward mid-Channel where dimly-lighted buoys tossed at the entrances to ten "approach lanes".

Dusk closed down on the Channel at a little after ten. A south-west wind set briskly across the tide and lifted the sea into a choppy swell. By midnight a full moon, rarely seen among patches of scudding cloud, had climbed above the horizon. Beneath it the dark face of the Channel was combed by twenty lines of red and white lights, winking faintly at one-mile intervals along the port and starboard boundaries of the ten lanes. Between the lights the ribbons of dark water were restless with shadowy movement, churned by an endless series of wakes whose ragged "V"s pointed steadily southward toward Baie de la Seine.

The columns of ships were speckled with the faint gleams of station-keeping lights, for this massive force had little to fear either from underwater or the sky. Far about it squadrons of destroyers and frigates fended off the U-boats. The allied air force had nearly destroyed the *Luftwaffe*. Orders were that no passing aircraft should be fired on, as it was almost certain to be friendly. The many engines droning overhead were those of bombers bound for the enemy coast. In an hour or so there would be a deeper, longer-sustained roar as transport planes and planes towing long strings of troop-carrying gliders began to pass over with the men of the parachute divisions.

Among the ships moving southward in the ten lanes were many ships of Canada. There were many more with the "screening forces", the patrols flung out to the east and west in the Bay of Biscay and the Channel and the North Sea. Canadian ships were still moving down along the coasts of England with reinforcement convoys bound for the assembly area. Far to the west in the Atlantic, hundreds of Canadian ships sailed along the convoy routes which had fed this strength to Britain. And almost at the beaches themselves now, far ahead of the approaching columns, sixteen Canadian minesweepers were at work on a task from which not many of their men expected to return.

10. The Assault

THE lights which greeted the ten columns of ships as they entered the approach channels had been set in place by flotillas of minesweepers sailing five miles ahead of them. Each flotilla had to clear one channel in the great mine-barrier which the Germans had laid in front of the beaches. At one-mile intervals as the sweepers moved inward they had dropped lighted "danbuoys" or markers anchored by weights and wires, along the borders of each lane.

Each of the flotillas was of ten ships and six of the Canadian Bangors were distributed among British flotillas. *Canso* worked in Channel 1. *Guysborough, Kenora, Vegreville,* and *Georgian* were in Channel 2, and *Thunder* was in Channel 4. In Channel 3, however, *Caraquet, Fort William, Wasaga, Cowichan, Minas, Malpeque, Bayfield, Milltown, Blairmore,* and *Mulgrave* made up an all-Canadian flotilla, the 31st.

Like their mates in the other ships, the men of the 31st Flotilla had had long years of drab work along the coast of Canada. In February they had come to England to be trained and to have their ships fitted out for the work of invasion. At 5.35 on the afternoon of June 5 they had sailed from the Isle of Wight. By early evening, in company with the other flotillas, they were in sight of the French coast and at seven o'clock in the evening they entered the minefield.

They were about thirty miles off shore as they began their work. They were to clear a lane twelve hundred yards wide. *Caraquet* led the formation with each ship astern of her sailing a little to the right of the one ahead. They were "staggered" in this way so that they would not become entangled in their "sweeps", the long, saw-toothed cables which ran out behind each ship, dragging a little below the surface. German mines lay a little under water where the hull of a ship would strike and explode them as it passed over. They were anchored to the bottom with weights and held in position by wires attached to the weights. They were usually designed to explode only under water and became harmless as they reached the surface. The cables of the sweepers were intended to cut across their mooring wires and bring them bobbing up.

German shore batteries were all along the coast. As the ships moved inward they began to come in range. It seemed impossible that they had not been sighted, but there was no puff of smoke from those grey cliffs nor any scream of shells. Neither was there any time to watch and listen, for minesweeping is always anxious work and this was one of the most difficult jobs which sweepers had ever done. The navigation of the ships had to be exact, since every foot of the channel must be covered. The long cables of the sweeps had to be kept always in position. On the afterdecks of the ships which were to set out lights there were great piles of buoys, floats, weights, shackles, and coils of wire. Each danbuoy had to go overside at the correct moment, weighted with two concrete blocks shackled to about six hundred feet of wire. It would be a marker for a line of approaching ships, and even one buoy out of place might delay or confuse a whole column.

It was nearly full dark as the 31st Flotilla finished sweeping the approach channel. The ships were now about eight miles inside the minefield and a little more than twenty miles from the coast. The next part of the work was to sweep the "assault channel" which turned a little toward the west and ran in toward the beaches for another eighteen miles. By twenty minutes after midnight this had been done. Next came the "boat lanes" which would carry the landing craft right in to the limit of deep water. At five minutes after one the ships turned directly for the beaches and ran to within a mile and a half of shore. They were in this position at three o'clock when the full moon, which had been riding above them lightly hidden by wind-driven clouds, broke through into a patch of clear sky. It lighted the sea for perhaps a minute. Then, as clouds drove over it again, men who had briefly remembered the dangers about them drew breath once more.

The ships, with their cables riding behind them, swung out to sea again. At the outer limit of the boat lanes they turned back and reswept to within two miles of shore. The miraculous silence of the enemy continued. The German batteries were holding their fire for fear of revealing their positions to Allied bombers. Unscarred by a single shell, the Bangors finished their work at 5.15 and went back up their channel to take the anchorage assigned to them.

They were none too quick about it. The assault-ships were already pouring down the channels, elbowing aside the returning sweepers. The men of the 31st Flotilla made out the shapes of the American battleships *Texas* and *Arkansas*, dimly outlined in the pre-dawn darkness. The British cruiser *Glasgow* moved by them, and then the French cruiser *Montcalm*. *Georges Leygues*, another French cruiser, passed so close to *Minas* that she had to go hard to starboard to avoid a collision. The whole vast force was now flooding inward down the ten aisles of sea, and each ship was moving to its allotted station.

Prince Henry and *Prince David*, each leading a column of other landing-ships, emerged from Channels 7 and 8. Reaching their positions seven miles off shore, they swung parallel to the coast and the ships behind swung with them. By 5.35 the nineteen vessels of the two columns were riding at anchor in an eerie half-dawn light, each an exact three hundred yards from the next.

Daylight broadened with a low cloud-base breaking up along the horizon. The ten lines of ships were still pouring inward from the north, but those which had already come down their channels had spread out eastward and westward along the coast for sixty miles. In front of every sector of the beaches the appointed vessels were swinging at anchor or moving into their places. The drone of returning bombers was heard overhead and the dim shore-line glowed and smoked from their bombs. In a few moments there was a dull roar from seaward and the first salvoes of battleships and cruisers, stationed far out, began to scream above the long lines of landing-ships.

The landing-ships themselves were now astir. On board *Prince Henry* and *Prince David* the crews of the assault-craft climbed into their places. In the troop-decks below, the waiting soldiers looked to their gear for the last time. They heard a scrape of static from the "loud hailer", the ships' public-address system. Then the voice came, brassy and hard, warning the groups of their approaching times: "Will move in . . . ten . . . minutes . . . will move in . . . five . . . minutes . . . will move . . . now."

The soldiers came up group by group from the troop-decks, climbed quietly into their places, and the assault-craft were lowered to the water. As the flights of craft were formed, each flight, led by a motor-gunboat, began the seven-mile trip. All along the front of Baie de la Seine, flotillas, flights, and forces merged into one vast inward movement, a low disturbance on the water crawling raggedly toward shore.

From behind the assault-craft, as they moved in, came the steady rumble of the bombardment. Passing salvoes screamed overhead. Before them, already at the edge of shallow water, the terrible rocket-firing ships were blasting lanes through beach obstacles and any defences in their way. Threading between the rocket-ships came craft which plunged up on the sand unloading the Avre tanks of the Royal Engineers to churn up minefields and knock down barriers in the path of the troops. Still other craft came close behind the Avres, spilling out men in water five feet deep. German machine-guns stuttered and fire churned the water about them as they went to work setting off mines and clearing beach obstructions.

Neither they nor all the gun-fire before them could do much to lessen the dangers of the man-made reefs which lined the beaches for a half-mile off shore. Just visible at the half-tide mark were heavy steel barriers, eight feet wide by ten feet high, projecting from the bottom. Next behind

them were lines of sharp wooden stakes driven deep in the sand. Behind the stakes were great steel prongs which would rip the bottom out of any vessel passing over them. Mines were hung on the prongs, other mines were strewn on the bottom between them, and nearest inshore in the breaking surf were rows of concrete blocks hung with more mines and with live shells.

As the assault-craft came to within a mile of shore the bombardment from sea rumbled into silence. Through a screen of spray the men in the craft caught occasional glimpses of sand and rock, of the grey humps of German pillboxes and gun emplacements and of woods beyond. Then, at twenty-seven minutes after eight, the first flights plunged for the beaches. The awful quiet which had followed the bombardment burst into a roar of mortar and machine-gun fire, punctuated by exploding mines and the crash of boats tearing out their bottoms.

By nine o'clock the shock-troops had been delivered. With them had come the vehicle-carrying craft, pouring out tanks, jeeps, trucks, and self-propelled guns. The assault wave had smashed its way in over all obstacles, reckless of loss. Along the length of the shore, swimming and drowning men, overturned tanks, craft sagging in shallow water or hung at sickening angles on pronged obstructions, were the sights which greeted the approaching wave of the reinforcements.

They were coming in now, carried by the larger landing-craft which had crossed the channel under their own power. There were twenty-nine Canadian craft among the hundreds making up the wave. Half a mile off shore the first four of the Canadians took their bearings on the spire of a little church in the distance. At 9.10, spotting what seemed to be a gap in the rows of obstacles peering through the surf, they went in for the beach at full speed.

The first two craft ground up on the rocky shore almost undamaged. The third, stopped dead by a concrete block, reared up with a great hole gashed in her side and dumped out her men in four feet of water. The fourth, charging through the shallows, had most of her bow blown off by a mine. Fire splattered the water, tanks and trucks were blazing, and mines were exploding on every side. Yet within ten minutes all but a dozen of the nearly seven hundred men carried by the four craft were moving off into the smoke of battle.

It was raging now all along the beaches. By noon wrecked craft lined the shore, masses of equipment were burning at the water's edge and thousands of men, tanks and guns were milling around in apparent confusion. The appearance was deceptive. The landings had gone amazingly well. The footholds were being taken and held. Casualties among the troops were lighter than expected, and naval casualties were even lighter. Not one Canadian sailor had been killed and only a handful wounded. Many of the wrecked landing-craft would soon be repaired, and even now some of them were turning back for England.

Of the eight assault-craft which *Prince David* sent in, only one came back to her. All but one of *Prince Henry*'s had returned by noon. By early afternoon both Canadian ships, swinging at anchor with their group, were busy on other work. The first of the wounded were coming out from the beaches.

Prince David took on board fifty-eight men and *Prince Henry* fifty-six, lowering them on stretchers to the sick bays and hospitals set up in the ward-rooms. As the stretchers swung down all excitement over the success of the landings was quickly subdued. Many of the wounded, soaked, blood-stained and covered with sand from the beaches, died as they were being hoisted on board, or before they could be laid on an operating table. Others lay back, their eyes closed, their faces grey-white, drawing deeply on cigarettes offered them by the watching sailors, while still others chattered with the feverish cheerfulness of shell-shocked men. Throughout the afternoon and night doctors and chaplains cared for the living or gave the last rites to those for whom men could do no more.

Fortress Europe had been breached. The great tide of men and ships and weapons had poured onto the coast of France. It would never be turned back, but no man could know that on June 6, 1944. Beyond that fringe of captured shore there were mighty armies waiting. At sea the last thrusts of a desperate enemy still remained to be dealt with.

11. Time's Revenges

At four o'clock on the afternoon of June 6, *Haida* and *Huron*, having spent an uneventful D-Day on patrol with British destroyers, returned to Plymouth for fuel. For a moment there was no word of enemy ships in their area and only a cloud of hopeful rumours from Baie de la Seine, 250 miles to the south-east.

Within an hour or so the situation had changed. Plymouth, at the south-western tip of England, looked down toward the Bay of Biscay and was the base for destroyers guarding the Channel mouth. A signal arrived at Plymouth in the early evening reporting that three German destroyers were heading up the Bay. They were powerful ships of the Narvik class, larger than Tribals, and they were believed to be heading for Brest, across the Channel from Plymouth on the German-held coast of France. In Brest another German destroyer was waiting to join them, and the aim of the combined force would be to enter the Channel and attack the invasion ships.

Six ships of the 10th Destroyer Flotilla were already on patrol in the Channel mouth and at 10.45 the next morning *Haida* and *Huron* joined them. About five in the afternoon came a signal reporting that the Narviks had arrived off Brest and had been joined by *Tjerk Hiddes*, a captured Dutch destroyer now manned by Germans. It was very likely that the attempt to enter the Channel would be made that night.

The 10th Flotilla was made up of the British destroyers *Tartar, Ashanti, Eskimo,* and *Javelin,* the Polish destroyers *Blyskawica* and *Piorun,* and the two Canadians. When the signal arrived it was patrolling a little inside the Channel. It was now ordered onto a series of courses which would take it out into the Bay and south-westerly across the route of the German ships.

By ten o'clock in the evening the force had reached its first position, just in the Channel mouth and north of the French coast. It was moving in two columns about two miles apart. At the head of the first column sailed *Tartar,* the senior ship, leading *Ashanti, Haida,* and *Huron. Blyskawica,* leading the second column, was followed by *Eskimo, Piorun,* and *Javelin.* The zig-zagging, twenty-knot sweep to the south-westward now began.

For several hours there was no sign of an enemy. The blacked-out ships steamed on with only the rare glint of a signal-lamp passing between them. Throughout the afternoon and evening *Haida's* and *Huron's* men, like the men in the other ships, had gone to the showers in groups, scrubbing themselves with strong-smelling soap. They had changed their underclothing to guard against any infection which might enter their bodies with a wound. Now they were at action stations, moving side by side with the men of the Royal Navy and the men of ravished Poland.

Look-outs in their windy stations combed the dark sea. Below them in stuffy cabins men sat or stood before brightly-lighted instrument-panels, their hands busy, their eyes alert. Steel-helmeted gunners waited by the hatches of the opened magazines, looking like ghosts with white canvas gloves running up their forearms to protect them from the flash of the guns, and white canvas masks dropping from beneath their helmets to their shoulders, leaving only their eyes and noses to be seen. Dark figures high above them on the bridges spoke in occasional tense murmurs, bent over dials and the mouthpieces of speaking-tubes and telephones as the ceaseless flow of orders and reports passed back and forth between the nerve-centres and the eyes and brains of the ships.

In the sick bays and ward-rooms medical officers and attendants cleared extra space and laid out their instruments, drugs, and plasma. Mess decks and officers' cabins were deserted. Magazines lay open with their stories half-read. Unfinished letters lay with the pens on the paper. From the swaying bulkheads photographs and pin-ups still looked down, but no men looked back at them. Seamen off watch sat or lay or slept beside their stations, on deck, along dimly-lighted companion-ways, at the foot of ladders, or wherever there was room for a stretched-out or coiled-up body. Deep beneath them the throbbing engines, nursed by the men who would have the least chance of escape from disaster, sent the destroyers weaving onward. Far ahead of them the invisible, unheard radar-beams, searching out and returning with their numberless echoes, sent the running green ribbon of each operator's dial rising in jagged crests and falling away into troughs like the sea about it.

The weather was cloudy and rough, with sudden rain-squalls shutting off the view ahead. Banks of low cloud were confusing the radar "blips". Not until one o'clock did the first promising echoes begin to come in. First one contact, then another, and finally a third and fourth became definite. By 1.20 it was clear that four vessels were approaching from the south-west at a speed of twenty-six knots.

They were still about six miles off. The 10th Destroyer Flotilla continued toward them through the squally night. As the range closed, *Tartar* ordered a turn to port to bring the force broadside-on to the enemy. The ships turned, the moon broke through the scudding clouds, and the camouflaged sides of the enemy stood out in the wan light. The straining eyes of look-outs fastened on the broken silhouettes glimmering in the distance. From British, Canadian, and Polish bridges the drone of ranges and bearings began.

It was now likely that the Germans would fire torpedoes. The allied ships, therefore, swung back directly toward them to reduce the size of the target. *Ashanti, Haida,* and *Huron* spread out behind *Tartar. Blyskawica's* division, two miles to seaward and a little astern, took up the same formation.

The enemy ships could now be seen turning away to port. The range had closed to two and a half miles. At 1.27 *Tartar, Ashanti, Haida,* and *Huron* opened fire, and a moment later flashes could be seen from the guns of *Blyskawica*'s brood. The leading German destroyer seemed to be running for the north, and *Tartar* ignored him. Closing to point-blank range but moving carefully for fear of torpedoes, she turned her fire on the second ship in the German line. *Ashanti* joined in this attack and almost at once the salvoes from the British ships began to land on their target. *Haida* took on the third enemy ship and *Huron* the fourth. Already a great mass of greyish-yellow smoke had settled on the sea as the Germans scattered behind their screen.

For a moment *Tartar* lost her target in the murk and swung off to give *Haida* a hand. She had hardly done so when the leader of the German ships came doubling back from the north and rained shells on her. Three direct hits put seventeen of her men out of action and set the ship afire. For a few minutes her guns replied to the German but soon the blaze amidships forced her to break off. She headed for the north, away from the wind which was fanning the flames, while damage-control parties fought for the ship's life.

Meanwhile the other ships were beginning to lose track of each other. Star-shell burst high above the low-hanging clouds, throwing light on them but little on the sea. Shells were bursting, flames were lifting from several decks, and smoke was everywhere. *Ashanti* had left the ship she was attacking and gone to help *Tartar*, but just as she was nearing the damaged destroyer, her former target, the *Tjerk Hiddes*, came up through the gloom on her port bow.

The enemy destroyer was in trouble, stopped or going very slowly. *Ashanti* turned on it with a salvo of four torpedoes, one of which caught it astern while a second blew off a length of its bow. Although mortally hit, the stoutly-built ship showed no inclination to sink. *Ashanti* circled it, pouring in a heavy fire and receiving some fire in return. Flames and smoke wreathing about the vessel were continually hiding it from view. It must have been an inferno from end to end, but one of its guns scored a last hit on *Ashanti.* Then firing ceased and some of its men could be seen climbing over the sides. At 2.40, after a brave last hour, *Tjerk Hiddes* blew up with an explosion which lifted a great plume of flame above the evil fog.

The ships which *Haida* and *Huron* had attacked were making off very fast to the south-west behind a heavy smoke-screen. *Haida*'s target drew away from her and she turned her guns onto the destroyer which *Huron* was pursuing. The Canadian ships drew together, each of them scoring hits on the enemy and receiving a steady fire in reply. *Huron* fired torpedoes but failed to hit and a little later the German, running southward, suddenly swung east. It was a risky move for him, since it took him squarely across a minefield which the British had laid in the area, but it saved him for a time. The Canadian ships had orders to go round the minefield and the long detour put them out of touch with their enemy. At 2.15 they gave up the chase and turned back to the other battle.

Tartar was now out of action. *Tjerk Hiddes* had sunk. One German had escaped *Haida* to the west and was being chased by the ships of *Blyskawica*'s division. Another had outrun *Huron* and *Haida* to the south-east and the location of the fourth ship was doubtful. As the two Canadians steered back toward the north, however, it was soon to be revealed.

Haida was the first to get a radar contact, six miles off on her port bow. It seemed hardly to be moving, and at first she thought it was the damaged *Tartar*. Closing on the contact, *Haida* and *Huron* made out through the darkness the shape of a destroyer moving north-west at slow speed. They flashed a signal demanding the ship's identity and got a reply they could not understand. Bringing their guns to bear, they repeated the challenge. Again the reply was meaningless. By now the Canadian destroyers were within a mile of the stranger and they were still in doubt. It could very well be *Tartar* lying there, silent and dead on the water with her signalling-gear out of action. As they crossed warily astern, however, all doubts were resolved. The ship swung suddenly south, spewed out a cloud of smoke, and took off at high speed.

For a short time he disappeared into the dark. *Haida* and *Huron* went flat out after him. The German was one of the big Narviks, and his gunnery was good. Star-shell burst accurately above the Canadians and high explosive lifted straddling splashes in the water about them. The German was making thirty-one knots and pulling a little ahead. He was steering south and east, evidently hoping to take refuge in the Channel Islands. *Haida* and *Huron*, still astern to the north, were running to head him off.

At 3.11 the enemy swung more to the east, and the new course took him across the same minefield through which the earlier destroyer had escaped. Once again the Canadian ships had to go round, and for a time it seemed that they were in for another disappointment. The range increased to over ten miles and finally radar contact was lost.

At four o'clock *Haida* and *Huron*, having circled the mine-field and lost their echo, were steering north-easterly some thirty miles off the French coast. They held on for eleven discouraging minutes with little clue as to the German's whereabouts. Then at 4.12 an echo came. The Narvik was nine miles due east of them and running for the port of Cherbourg, beyond the Channel Islands.

The Canadians worked up to thirty-one knots and set after him. With a considerable start, the Narvik might have made Cherbourg in safety. Instead, for some reason which was never explained, he altered back to the south-west at 4.32. The change of course put *Haida* and *Huron* in a position to cut him off. Sharply altering their own course, they steered in across his line of advance and were waiting for him at five o'clock as he ran out from the fringes of another minefield.

The Narvik found the two Tribals some four miles off on his starboard bow, and the guns began to bark as the three ships ran on parallel courses headed for the French coast. Salvoes from both Canadian ships plunged onto the target immediately. Splashes of flame began to appear along the German's decks and his return fire became erratic. He held his course and speed unchanged, and at 5.17 ran in among the rocks of the coast and hard aground. *Haida* and *Huron* followed to within three miles and kept up their fire until he was completely ablaze and helpless. Then, leaving behind them a dense column of smoke against a brightening sky, they turned back for Plymouth.

There were to be no more German threats from the Bay of Biscay. Here, as in the Channel and the North Sea, allied ships crushed every attempt to harry the forces of invasion. From Baie de la Seine the great armies moved inward toward the Rhine, and when the Tribals returned to Biscay waters a month later they were on other work. Isolated German garrisons, clinging to ports along the French coast, had to be starved out by sinking the ships which supplied them.

On August 5 the British cruiser *Bellona* sailed from Plymouth leading a force which included *Tartar*, *Haida*, *Ashanti*, and *Iroquois*, which had now replaced *Huron*. The force passed down the Biscay coast leaving Saint-Nazaire behind them and had just drawn abreast of the little island, Ile d'Yeu, when very-long-range radar contacts began to come in. The echoes grew clearer and were soon identified as those of enemy ships. A supply convoy was passing between Ile d'Yeu and the coast, working slowly out toward sea.

For two hours the British force stalked the slow merchantmen and their escorts, keeping carefully at a distance until the Germans had moved out from shore. Then, at ten minutes after midnight, the destroyers drove in at twenty-five knots between the convoy and the land.

Bellona remained to seaward, and at 12.33 her first starshell burst above the convoy. There were seven German ships, and in less than twelve minutes six were ablaze and sinking. One made its escape. *Iroquois* accounted for two of the vessels, *Tartar* and *Ashanti* between them for three. *Haida* had her first target, a minesweeper, settling to the bottom within four minutes of opening fire, and some of her salvoes had landed on one of the other vessels when she suffered the worst mishap of her brilliant career. A shell exploded as it was going into the breech of one of her after guns, wrecking the turret, killing two of the gunners and wounding eight more.

The damage to *Haida* was serious but not crippling, and the night was still young. The force reformed and turned back to the north. As the ships passed Saint-Nazaire, radar echoes indicated another convoy creeping close to the coast. For the moment it could not be attacked. It was moving through a narrow, rocky channel with minefields laid on both sides, and there was no room for the destroyers to manoeuvre in the shallow water.

The convoy, however, would soon have to come out from shelter. The destroyers swung out to sea, waited for fifteen minutes, and then came in again. They found the merchant vessels just clear of the shallows but already alarmed and turning back. Opening with star-shell and high explosive and closing to a range of three miles, the destroyers saw their hits registering in jagged red splashes. Then salvoes from German shore batteries began to come down and the ships, neatly silhouetted by the moon, had to move out to sea. They came in again, got away a few salvoes, and again withdrew. Twice more they did the same thing. For forty minutes, alternately drawing away from the shore batteries and boring in on the ships, they harried the convoy as it crawled back toward the coast. They had sunk two and damaged others when dawn brought the threat of air attack and they had to retire to Plymouth.

On August 7 and again on August 14 British and Canadian ships returned to Biscay waters, destroying three more German convoys. Eight days later, on August 22, the work rose to its climax. This time *Iroquois* sailed in company with the British cruiser *Mauritius* and the British destroyer *Ursa*. As the ships swept down from Plymouth they detected a first convoy about midnight. Standing off from shore they gave it time to reach deep water, then cut in on the landward side, trapping it. Star-shell flared and the rapid salvoes burst among the ships. Three of the vessels drove in for the shoals, ablaze from end to end, and before their keels grated over the rocks a fourth had blown up.

Two hours later, while the earlier ships were still burning along the coast, another convoy was detected. Followed at long range by *Iroquois*'s radar, it was stalked, suddenly lighted by star-shell and overwhelmed with fire. Two of the vessels sank. Two more, running in to beach themselves, collided and burst into flames. One of these turned over and disappeared. The other rode high up onto the rocks and remained there, lifting jagged tongues of flame into the sky. As the cruiser and the two destroyers turned back for Plymouth in the early dawn they left behind them three ships sunk and five blazing along the beach. In September of 1941 *Iroquois*'s captain, as senior officer of the escort for Convoy SC-42, had seen sixteen of his ships go down in Greenland waters. The whirligig of time had brought in its revenges.

12. Liberation

FOUR days later, on the afternoon of August 26, *Iroquois* was passing Ile d'Yeu again. She was still scarred and grim from the last battle. There were shrapnel gashes in her hull. Her paint-work was burnt away and the rails along her decks were bent and twisted from the blast of her guns. She was on patrol with *Mauritius,* and she was once more looking for trouble.

Her look-outs reported a small boat putting out from the direction of Ile d'Yeu. People in the boat seemed to be making an effort to attract the destroyer's attention. *Iroquois* slowed down and brought her guns to bear, while men with binoculars watched the approaching craft.

A girl in slacks, sweater, and a beret was standing in the boat waving a handkerchief frantically. Three or four men seated along the thwarts were beckoning and calling. *Iroquois* came to a stop while *Mauritius* waited a mile or so to seaward. The boat was allowed to come alongside, ropes were tossed over and the girl, followed by her companions, clambered on board.

She was Mademoiselle Anne-Marie Gaston, a schoolteacher on Ile d'Yeu. She was black-eyed, dark-skinned, eager and determined. She spoke English, and a great deal of it. The men with her were some of the leading citizens. The German garrison of the island, they said, had left the night before. The Maquis, the French underground fighters, were now in control. They had information for the allied ships and they were very short of food. Could a party be sent ashore to consult with the French officers, and could some provisions be spared?

Signals passed between the captain of *Iroquois* and the captain of *Mauritius*. It seemed that this might be a chance to gain valuable information about the Germans. It was decided to put a party from *Iroquois* ashore. The ship herself would continue on patrol with *Mauritius* and return for the men next day.

Every man in the Tribal was an eager volunteer, but only two officers and three signalmen could be spared. Lieutenant J. S. Saks went in command. Engineer-Lieutenant Richard Scrivener, a French-speaking Montrealer, went as interpreter and the three signalmen were Petty Officer R. Mulligan, Telegraphist J. Chevalier, who also spoke French, and Signalman G. A. Sheppard. Signalling gear was loaded into the boat so that the shore-party could keep in touch with the ship. Flour, canned meat, milk, sugar, chocolate bars, and cigarettes followed. The boat, low in the water with its passengers, gear, and provisions, put in for the island as *Iroquois* swung to sea.

Mademoiselle Gaston warned the Canadians to be prepared for a welcome. Even so, as they set foot on shore, they nearly went down under a cheering, weeping, kissing multitude. They were carried shoulder-high to the town hall. They met the officers of the Maquis and arranged for the distribution of the food they had brought. The smiling underground fighters brought out German maps and captured orders and made sketches showing the location of German shore batteries all along the coast. And now, they asked, what more could be done for the Canadians?

The shore-party requested a place to set up its signalling equipment, and was taken first to the lovely old church. Mulligan climbed up inside the tower and was nearly brained when one of the excited crowd below decided to ring the bell. The church tower was not a suitable place for the signallers. Officials of the town then produced an ancient car which had not run since the war began. They brought out a few gallons of gasoline, stolen pint by pint from the Germans. A wildly rejoicing fisherman took over as chauffeur and, tooting an incessant V-for-Victory on his horn, rocketed them up the steep streets of the town to a signal-tower standing about three miles away.

The door of the tower had been blocked, but the sailors and their hosts climbed in through a low window. In the top loft of the tower the signalmen set up their wireless equipment, while below them in the dusty, echoing, ground-level compartment the two officers spread out the maps and papers they had been given. The townspeople withdrew to let the Canadians work undisturbed, but toward evening Mademoiselle Gaston came again. A small banquet had

been prepared in the town. Would the Canadians come now and eat? Regretfully the Canadians had to decline. There was much to do and they had not yet reported to their ship. Mademoiselle Gaston left, disappointed. The sailors, munching their lean rations of bread and jam, went on working by flashlights which were the only light they had. About midnight the voice of one of the signalmen boomed down through the dark tower, reporting that he had made contact with *Iroquois*.

At one o'clock in the morning the drowsing men heard voices outside. They turned their flashlights on the low window and were just in time to see Mademoiselle Gaston step over the ledge. Behind her, solemnly one by one and all in their Sunday best, came fifteen ladies and gentlemen of the village. No one noticed what the men wore. But the black silk of the ladies' dresses rustled softly, and standing high and graceful on each head was the exquisite starched lace "coif" of the Breton woman.

Each of the party carried a basket. They had walked the three miles from town with the provisions for the banquet. There were cakes and wine and fruits. There were lobsters and sardines. There were the long-legged crabs which made the waters of the island famous among fishermen. There were bottles of champagne which had been "requested" from the hotel of a man who had collaborated with the Germans.

The long table was cleared of papers. The food was spread out. Men gathered wood to make a fire. At first the Canadians were a little bug-eyed and the townsfolk rather solemn. But the stiffness melted away. There was much laughter, and there were brave attempts at speech-making in unknown tongues. There were toasts to Canada, toasts to France, toasts to Ile d'Yeu, toasts to *Iroquois*. And afterwards the people spoke a little of their late conquerors.

The Germans, they said in their pleasantly contemptuous French way, had been "not *too* disagreeable". But they had become sullen and gloomy as their days began to run out. They had listened unhappily to the sound of gun-fire rolling in from the sea, and had waited for convoys which did not come. Yesterday they had destroyed a few buildings and gun-emplacements, looted the little post office of its five thousand francs, stolen a few fishing boats and set off for the German garrison on the mainland. So, shabbily, the Nazi dream of glory had faded from Ile d'Yeu.

Dinner ended, the townspeople left, and the Canadians worked on in watches through the night. *Iroquois* signalled that a boat would land for them on the seaward side of the island. Early in the morning they prepared to go.

The ancient automobile arrived for them, but with it arrived the head of Ile d'Yeu's French war veterans' association. There were allied airmen buried on the island. It was the first Sunday of the liberation and a ceremony was to be held at the graves. Would the Canadians march with the war veterans and the townspeople?

It was a request which could not be refused. The five sailors fell in with the French veterans and over a thousand of the villagers. At their head was a fine bugle band. They marched first to the graves of the airmen whose bodies had been recovered from the sea. The graves stood in a row, carefully tended, each with a neat headstone. The men came to attention. The bugles rang out in a long, solemn call. There was a minute's silence. Then the march went on to the graves of the French war dead and the ceremony was repeated.

The procession moved away from the cemetery and came into the town again. Just before ranks were broken the Commandant insisted that the senior officer of the Canadian party address the crowd. Saks tried to get off with the announcement he had been authorized to make: the waters which had been forbidden to the fishermen all through the war were now open to them again. The news was greeted with cheers, but still a speech was demanded. Saks made a brave attempt with what he could remember of his high school French. "Lord, sir," whispered Chevalier as he paused to draw breath, "if you only knew what you're saying!"

Again out of the crowd Mademoiselle Gaston appeared. Her boat was loaded with the Canadians' equipment and was waiting to take them round the island to where the ship's boat would land. The Canadians followed her to the boat and were startled to find among their heaped-up gear a huge white cake decorated with the inscription: "Vive la France, Canada, Britain, and America". Baked with some of the flour brought from *Iroquois*, it had been intended for last night's banquet. Now, since it could not be carried the three miles from town, the Canadians must take it with them.

They put off and came round the island to where the ship's boat was waiting. It was almost hidden under masses of flowers. A crowd of islanders stood about it, cheering the sailors who were trying to dance with the girls of Ile d'Yeu on the sandy beach. Gear was transferred, farewells were made, and a wave of cheering followed the boat to sea.

For Canadian sailors it was a glimpse of freedom restored, a foretaste of victory. Churchill's promise had been fulfilled, and they had had a share in the fulfilment. Over the long sea road and in God's good time the new world with all its power and might had stepped forth to the rescue and liberation of the old.

13. Black Flags

By the spring of 1945 the war with Germany was almost won. Four million allied soldiers had been delivered to the continent of Europe. They were pouring across the Rhine from the west, while from the east the Russian advance was a pillar of cloud by day and of fire by night. Tremendous fleets of allied bombers ranged over the last strongholds of the Nazi enemy, pounding them to rubble. Mass raids on German shipyards destroyed in seconds the work of months and years. In the U-boat bases the debris of barracks, docks, cranes, and machine-shops lay strewn above the deep steel and concrete shelters from which the sea-fighters were controlled.

Yet still new boats were built and still they came to sea. On the winter Atlantic, in those first months of 1945, it seemed that the battle was resuming with all its old ferocity. On January 4 two ships were torpedoed twenty miles off

Halifax. A few days later two more went down a little to the south. In late February our corvette *Trentonian* was sunk by a torpedo in British waters, and on April 16 the Bangor minesweeper *Esquimalt* went down in the very approaches to Halifax harbour.

The ship had been on patrol only a few miles out from the coast. A torpedo struck her on the starboard side, killing many men with the explosion. Tons of sea-water flooded in through a great hole to drag the Bangor down with sickening speed. The lifeboats were under water and flooded on their davits before they could be released. Four carley floats got away and the survivors of the explosion dragged themselves onto the rafts or clung to handholds on the rubber sides. Through six hours of waiting, icy waves washed over the shocked and exhausted men. By the time their sister ship *Sarnia* arrived, thirty-nine were dead or missing out of a crew of sixty-five.

April wore to its close with no apparent reduction either in the numbers of the U-boats or the spirit of their men. There came instead reports that new wolf-packs were forming. The reports were not true, there would be no more wolf-packs; but the many captains sailing alone were still as active, still as dangerous as ever. There was something aimless and convulsive about the vigour they displayed, as well there might be. Most of their bases were cut off by allied armies or bombed to pieces by the allied air force. From their few remaining control-centres the orders reaching them grew broken and confused. The great wireless transmitters were toppling, the shell-shocked operators were falling at their posts. Everywhere around the world darkness was closing on

the underwater navy, yet the great sea-beast displayed a
terrible vitality. Its far-reaching tentacles, almost severed
now from the battered head, still writhed and struck.

With the first days of May came rumours of German
surrender. It was hard for the worn men in the ships to
believe them. On May 5 an American freighter was torpedoed
off Rhode Island. On May 6 an American destroyer, circling
the position, brought a familiar gush of U-boat wreckage to
the surface. On May 7 a submarine was attacked in the
approaches to New York harbour, and later in the same day
two merchant vessels and a minesweeper were torpedoed in
the Irish Sea. On the morning of May 8 a cargo vessel was
sunk off the Belgian port of Ostend, and at 8.21 that night
a British escort group began an attack on a U-boat to the
north of Bristol Channel. An hour and forty minutes later,
while wreckage from this attack was streaming to the surface
in the midst of a great lake of oil, the sea-war officially ended.

At one minute after ten on the night of May 8 the German
High Command broadcast an order to all its U-boats at sea.
The order had been dictated by allied officers and contained
the following instructions:

A. Surface and remain surfaced.

B. Report your position and number to the nearest
   British, United States, Canadian or Soviet wireless station.

C. Fly black or blue flag by day and burn navigation
   lights by night.

D. All ammunition to be thrown overboard; all warheads to be removed from torpedoes.

E. Make all signals in plain language.

F. Refrain from scuttling or in any way damaging your U-boat.

G. Report your position, course and speed every eight hours.

H. Proceed by direct route to the nearest allied port.

The signal was repeated two hours later, and again at the next two-hour interval and the next. It was to circle the globe monotonously for the next three weeks, and it was to be followed by warning messages to the boats which had not replied.

One by one, most of the boats of the underwater navy rose to the surface. At 6.39 on the morning of May 9 Canadian naval wireless stations heard the position report of *U-805* in mid-Atlantic. Twenty-five minutes later an unidentified boat reported herself at the south-west tip of England, and a minute after that *U-1105* spoke from north-west of Ireland. At intervals through the day followed more reports, from the western Atlantic, from the mouth of the English Channel, from north-east and north-west of the Shetland Islands, and from north of Scotland. Eight boats reported on May 10, six on the eleventh, and from that time on the welcome messages dwindled to a trickle of two or three daily.

The behaviour of the surrendering boats was in most cases correct. The commander of *U-532*, however, proved to be an invincible optimist. On May 11, from far north of the British Isles, he signalled his control-centre at Bergen on the Norwegian coast asking if last-minute sinkings could be credited and if promotion would follow as usual. It was May 15 before Bergen replied, with the permission of allied officers, that there would be no more promotions. U-532 never got the message. By that time she was tied to a jetty in a Scottish port, a captive with her wireless sealed.

At six o'clock on the evening of May 10 an American Liberator sighted U-889 two hundred and fifty miles southeast of the coast of Newfoundland, travelling on the surface and flying a black flag. The Canadian frigates *Dunvegan* and *Rockcliffe* were called away from a convoy to meet the boat. They took station on either side of the German and gave him a course for Shelburne, Nova Scotia. On the way they were relieved by the frigates *Buckingham* and *Inch Arran*, and returned to the convoy they had left. Shortly after noon on the thirteenth, *Buckingham* and *Inch Arran*, with the black-flagged enemy riding between them, arrived off Shelburne. Launches came out to meet them carrying a boarding-party and at three o'clock formal surrender was made. The U-boat crew filed off their deck for the last time. A Canadian crew took over, hoisted the white ensign, and the boat was sailed into Shelburne harbour.

U-190, the boat which had sunk *Esquimalt*, was already on her way toward Bay Bulls, Newfoundland. She had reported her position on the evening of the eleventh, and the Canadian frigate *Victoriaville* with the corvette *Thorlock* had sailed to meet her. They came up shortly after midnight to find her surfaced and burning navigation lights. A boarding-party crossed over, and at two o'clock in the morning the U-boat captain signed a declaration typed on a letterhead of the Department of National Defence: "I hereby unconditionally surrender the German submarine U-190 to the Royal Canadian Navy."

On May 28 a signal went out around the world, discontinuing convoys in all the western oceans. One by one, as the signal reached the ships, points of red, green, and white began to twinkle among them. Then all lights were turned on. The convoys stood out like brilliant cities tossing on the dark seas, and men who had long sailed amid a hostile blackness found it hard to get used to the lights of peace.

Most of the Canadian ships in British waters were now homeward bound. Londonderry in Northern Ireland, lying twelve miles inland along the winding Foyle River, had been a favourite port for many of the escort groups, and they left it now with regret. "Make noise" was the signal of the port's commanding officer as one of the groups sailed out under a lowering dawn sky.

The ships were more than ready to obey. They let loose with guns pointed at the clouds and sirens blowing until the last ounce of steam died down. As they wound their way toward sea along the narrow Foyle the sun broke through upon the joyful racket and the rich, rolling fields bordering the inlet shone with all the green of Ireland.

Many of the men were already having a last look at the crops and browsing cattle, the white-washed cottages and the crumbling, green-grown ruins of the old castle. There was a general rush to the sides, however, as the order "All hands to port for Boom Hall" went out over the loud hailers. Boom Hall had been the war-time home of British and Canadian "Wrens" who did much of the navy's shore-side work at Londonderry. It was well within the sound of sirens from the Foyle, and the sight of waving girls lined along the river-bank had become as familiar as the sight of ships coming and going. Now the former "parties" of many a man at many a dance appeared again in an early-morning rush. Most of them had leaped from bed and put on whatever lay nearest to hand; some were taking out their curlers as they ran. Breathless and sometimes tearful, in bell-bottom trousers and raincoats over pyjamas, the Wrens of Londonderry waved good-bye to their sailors.

On down the Foyle the ships passed long lines of captured U-boats lying at anchor. An incoming Canadian escort group went by, back from a last convoy to Gibraltar. The bronzed men from the south grinned with envious surprise at the sight of girls on board the outgoing ships. Eight of the Canadian Wrens had been granted passage to Greenock as a victory gift. They roamed excitedly about the ships and, as one sailor reports, "a kindly tolerance was shown them by the salty veterans. They crowded the bridges, borrowed the binoculars, and ate the ships' food. *Glace Bay* fired eight rockets and two depth-charges for them. *Bowmanville* fired some more. They were roasted in engine-rooms and boiled in boiler-rooms as long-suffering engineer officers explained what made the wheels go round. This was the navy at play."

The war with Germany was over but there remained the war with Japan. Though few Canadian ships reached the Pacific before the fighting ended, many Canadians were already there. They were the men serving "on loan" in British ships or in the Fleet Air Arm of the Royal Navy. Altogether some four thousand Canadians served with the Royal Navy, very often on strange missions in remote corners of the world. From among them all one name stands out for lasting remembrance.

Robert Hampton Gray of Nelson, British Columbia, was a Fleet Air Arm pilot serving in the British carrier *Formidable*. On August 9, 1945, the planes of his squadron took off from the deck of the ship as it steamed along the west coast of Japan toward the port of Honshu. Only six days remained of the war, but the battering of Japanese ships, harbours, and naval bases was to go on until the cease-fire. Lying along the route to Honshu was the base of Onagawa, and it was the target of the planes as they wheeled into formation above the carrier.

Gray was a section commander of one of the flights. He had been commissioned as a sub-lieutenant at Kingston, Ontario, in December, 1940. He was twenty-seven years old and war was the only profession he had ever known. A week earlier, on August 2, he had sunk a Japanese destroyer and had been recommended for the Distinguished Service Cross. He had no knowledge of the award, however, as the sections streamed away and *Formidable* dwindled behind them into a moving speck on the sea.

As the flights approached the harbour of Onagawa five warships could be seen lying at anchor. From them and from the powerful batteries ringing the bay a curtain of anti-aircraft fire, steadily growing heavier, rose to meet the planes.

Fliers astern of Gray saw him go into a run aimed at one of the destroyers. As his plane swung onto an attacking course a cone of fire from ships and shore batteries centred on it. A first hit registered, then a second. A moment later streamers of flame began to bleed out astern of the aircraft.

It still held steadily to its course. Weaving and ablaze it bore down to within fifty yards of the destroyer before its bombs were seen to fall. One struck directly amidships, a second fell on or near alongside the target. The ship sank almost immediately, but before it disappeared Gray's riddled plane had dived into the waters of the bay.

The attack had been delivered with the cold precision of an instructor at a training school. It had been made with the skill born of five years' experience, and with a complete acceptance of the dangers. It was the work of a man who was prepared to offer everything he had to advance the cause he fought for.

Gray was the one man in the Canadian navy to receive the Victoria Cross. More than seventeen hundred others received British or foreign decorations. They were won on the Atlantic and the Mediterranean and in British waters. They were won by men of the landing-ships who took part in the invasion of southern France. They were won by destroyer men who went with the convoys bound for Murmansk and battled with the German surface navy in the high Arctic. They were won by men of the ships and landing-craft who took part in the invasion of Sicily and the liberation of Greece. The "gongs" were well earned, yet every man who was honoured knew that only the chances of battle had distinguished him from hundreds of other men equally deserving.

It was the same with the ships they served in. Canadian ships, alone or in company with other ships and planes, sank twenty-seven U-boats. They sank, captured, or destroyed forty-two enemy surface vessels. Yet the victories and the honours went to the lucky few, and were only the highlights of the battle. The greatest victory was the work of all.

During 2,060 days of war 25,343 merchant-ship voyages made under Canadian escort carried 181,643,180 tons of cargo to the United Kingdom. Over the bridge which the navy helped to build, some 90,000 tons of war supplies passed daily toward the battlefields of Europe.

There was a price to be paid in ships and men. *Fraser*, sunk off the coast of France in 1940, was a victim of the days of ruin and disaster. *Athabaskan* went down during the grim and confident sweeps before invasion. *Regina*, *Alberni*, and *Trentonian* were sacrificed in British waters. *Louisbourg* and *Weyburn* were a part of the cost of victory in the Mediterranean. Eight ships, *Bras d'Or*, *Otter*, *Raccoon*, *Charlottetown*, *Chedabucto*, *Shawinigan*, *Clayoquot*, and *Esquimalt*, were sunk in the defence of our own waters; and the six-year battle along the convoy routes of the North Atlantic claimed *Margaree*, *Levis*, *Windflower*, *Spikenard*, *Ottawa*, *Saint Croix*, *Valleyfield*, *Skeena*, and *Guysborough*. In these ships and in others, and in battles ranging over most of the world's seas, 1,797 Canadians lost their lives, 319 were wounded, and 95 became prisoners of war.

As men came out of the navy and laid their uniforms away

they found themselves faced with a new world. Many had still to go back to college or find themselves a first job. Little of what they had learned in war could be used in the days of peace. There was much to be changed, much to be learned and done in order to catch up and fit in with a life which had gone on in their absence. There were memories they could not share with anyone who had not known them, and shipmates they would not see often again. They would tell their stories to the "shore-side types" and find that no one laughed because they did not understand the navy talk. For some of them, old horrors would come back at night and they would lie awake a while. Everything would be a little lonely at first, a little strange.

Yet out of it all remained the abiding reward. "So long as memory lasts," said Angus L. Macdonald, the Navy Minister, in Parliament, "the recollection of those great days will be with them, and they will carry in their hearts forever the image of a gallant ship and the spell of the great sea."